go-to dinners

go-to dinners

a barefoot contessa cookbook

MAKE AHEAD

FREEZE AHEAD

PREP AHEAD

EASY

ASSEMBLED

ina garten

PHOTOGRAPHS BY QUENTIN BACON

CLARKSON POTTER/PUBLISHERS NEW YORK

Published in the United States by
Clarkson Potter/Publishers, an imprint
of Random House, a division of
Penguin Random House LLC, New York.
ClarksonPotter.com
RandomHouseBooks.com

Library of Congress Cataloging-in-Publication
Data is available on request.

ISBN: 978-1-9848-2278-9
Ebook ISBN: 978-1-9848-2279-6

Printed in China

Photographer: Quentin Bacon
Food Stylist: Christine Albano
Contributing Editor: Pam Krauss
Editor: Raquel Pelzel
Editorial Assistant: Bianca Cruz
Designer: Marysarah Quinn
Production Editor: Terry Deal
Production Manager: Kim Tyner
Compositor: Merri Ann Morrell
Copy Editor: Kathy Brock
Indexer: Elizabeth Parson
Marketer: Windy Dorresteyn
Publicist: Kate Tyler

10 9 8 7 6 5 4 3 2 1

First Edition

contents

thank you!

When I started writing cookbooks in 1997, I was afraid it would be a very solitary pursuit. It sounds like it would be, right? But instead I discovered it is, in fact, a team sport and I adore the people who work with me to ensure the books are beautiful, that the recipes work *every* time, and that the books are easy to use.

First of all, thank you to my wonderful longtime editor, Pam Krauss, who has been with me since 2001 and makes every book so much better. She also knows how to gently tell me something needs to be changed without hurting my feelings. Thanks to Clarkson Potter/Publishers, who has published every book since *The Barefoot Contessa Cookbook* in 1999. Thank you particularly to Marysarah Quinn for all the beautifully designed books and who kindly lets me be involved in the design process. Thanks also to the team at Potter: David Drake, Aaron Wehner, Francis Lam, Susan Corcoran, Kate Tyler, and Raquel Pelzel. I so admire all of you and am very grateful for your constant support.

Thank you also to the extraordinary people who come to work with me every day: Rose Brown, Kristina Felix-Ibarra, and Cindy Massey. Sarah Leah Chase writes her own wonderful cookbooks and helps me with mine. Thank you for making every day so much fun for me.

One of the happiest parts of writing cookbooks is photographing the food and, yet again, Quentin Bacon has taken the most amazing photographs with the assistance of Kristen Walther, and Christine Albano with Dylan Going prepared the gorgeous food. My dear friend, photographer Miguel Flores-Vianna, styled the photographs so beautifully. And thanks to Peter and Jennie Wallace and their gorgeous children, William, Caroline, and James, who came to cook and have dinner with me for the photographs. Thank you all for the wonderful days we spent together!

Thank you, too, to my amazing agent, Esther Newberg, who takes such good care of me. And finally, to my adorable husband, Jeffrey, who is always available to cheer me up and cheer me on. I'd have trouble getting out of bed every morning without your love and support.

introduction

"I love you, come for dinner!"

Isn't that the invitation we all want to hear? It promises an evening of good food, warm conversations, and the chance to share our lives with family and close friends. But to me, "come for dinner" is more than just an invitation to a meal; it's a celebration of community. Dinner nourishes our bodies, but it's the connection with people we love that nourishes our souls, and that's what I actually crave the most.

If the pandemic has taught me anything, it's how satisfying it is to be in the actual—rather than Zoom!—company of people we love. I need that closeness and connection more than anything else in my life; it gives me a reason to live. So when I say "Come for dinner!" it's really my way of saying "I love you, you matter to me." And of course you can expect a delicious meal, too!

It wasn't always that way for me. As a child, I dreaded dinnertime. My mother prepared food without enthusiasm (or much flavor) and my father was a stern taskmaster whose idea of dinner conversation was peppering me with questions about my school work until my stomach was tied in knots. As soon as it was over, I would rush back to the safety of my bedroom.

But that all changed when I married Jeffrey! All of a sudden, I had the freedom to create whatever kind of home I wanted and I knew one key to making that home a happy one was to have lots of good friends. So I threw a *lot* of dinner parties. I bought

Craig Claiborne's brilliant *The New York Times Cookbook* and spent my days trying out recipes and invited friends for dinner almost every week. I'm not sure my parties were all that great in the beginning (yes, I had a few disasters!) but I was so happy and Jeffrey was so supportive that it all helped me overcome my childhood dinnertime anxieties. I was learning not only how to cook but also how to create an atmosphere where friends could have a wonderful time together.

These days dinnertime has a different kind of importance for me. It's the end of the day, I've accomplished everything I need to get done, and now it's time to put work aside, relax, and have some fun. It's my time to connect with Jeffrey and my friends. I love when people walk in the door and the house smells good. I want each person to look forward to having something they love to eat. My idea of heaven is a Roast Chicken with Spring Vegetables (page 128) or Overnight Mac & Cheese (page 157) coming out of the oven and, for dessert, Beatty's Chocolate Cupcakes (page 233) or Lemon Meringue Squares (page 222) waiting on the counter to make everyone look forward to dessert. They're delicious, they're reliable, and they taste even better than you imagine.

OVERNIGHT MAC & CHEESE, PAGE 157

Restaurant food is wonderful but there is something soul-satisfying about making and eating a **real** home-cooked dinner right at your own kitchen table. Cooking a tried-and-true recipe that I know everyone will enjoy, maybe with some great music in the background, is like taking a deep yoga breath at the end of a stressful day. It just makes me feel really calm.

The pandemic has had a huge impact on what I think of as dinner—and what I look for in a "go-to" recipe. When I planned a party before the pandemic, it was always a multicourse extravaganza. But then the pandemic happened and everything seemed like so much more work. I started making simpler dinners for Jeffrey and me. I often made a lighter, easier, all-in-one-dinner like a Warm Vegetable & Grain Bowl (page 98) or Roasted Shrimp Panzanella (page 110). They were delicious, satisfying, and everything we needed and wanted for dinner. I began to question why I had been so rigid about what constituted dinner before—was this how I should be cooking for friends now? If I love eating this way, wouldn't my friends like it, too?

ROASTED SHRIMP PANZANELLA, PAGE 110

I also decided to relax my whole concept of what is considered "dinner." Why wouldn't the Easy Eggs in Purgatory (page 68) that I would normally make for Sunday brunch be great for dinner with big shards of toasted bread? Well, it turns out, it is! Or a big assembled platter of Provençal Orange Salad (page 113) with a rotisserie chicken that I picked up on the way home? It's a satisfying winter dinner that involves no cooking at all! A roast beef

BOURBON CHOCOLATE PECAN PIE, PAGE 230

sandwich from the deli might not feel like "dinner" but an indulgent Lobster & Avocado Sandwich (page 92) does. It's a bit unconventional but it sure is delicious!

And just because a recipe is easy to make, it shouldn't skimp on flavor or style. Summer Skillet with Clams, Sausage & Corn (page 145) is a classic summer meal but it's all made in one pot so there's almost no cleanup. My Salmon Teriyaki & Broccolini (page 150) takes less than 15 minutes to cook, and it all comes out of the oven together. For dessert, the Bourbon Chocolate Pecan Pie (page 230) is actually *better* with store-bought pie crust (and I'll tell you why!).

Cooking in the pandemic has also redefined my relationship with "leftovers." I used to hate leftovers. I just refused to eat them. First of all, eating the same thing two days in a row is boring, but more importantly, it's almost never as good as it was the first time around. The texture changes, the meat dries out, the flavors just aren't as bright. And if I don't look forward to dinner, I'm just not happy all day.

But there were also times during the pandemic when I had no idea if we could even *buy* more groceries. Instead of resigning myself to serving leftovers as is, I tried to think of new ways to be creative with what I had on hand. It became like a game to see how many different meals I could get out of the dinners I was cooking! I would make Chicken in a Pot with Orzo (page 131) one night and then add the shredded leftover chicken to Ravioli en Brodo (page 80) to make the soup even heartier for the next night. On Friday, I would serve Hasselback Kielbasa (page 139), then on Saturday, I'd dice the leftovers and add them to my Tuscan White Bean Soup (page 91) to make a hearty stew. I started planning ahead for these "Two-Fers," making enough Mussels with Saffron Cream (page 154) to have leftovers to serve as a treat with cocktails the next night. It wasn't boring; it was actually fun!

Cooking this way gave me the chance to focus on what constitutes a recipe that I turn to over and over again. Some recipes were just really easy to make and totally delicious. Others could be prepped largely in advance and thrown in the oven just before the meal, while still others could be made entirely ahead of time and reheated before serving. English Cream Scones (page 63) can be made in advance, frozen, and baked off for breakfast, tea in the afternoon, or breakfast for dinner. Smoked Salmon Quesadillas (page 34) can be assembled ahead and pan-fried for appetizers while Panettone Bread Pudding (page 212) can be put together early and baked off before dinner. My Chipotle Cheddar Crackers (page 42) can be frozen ahead and baked to serve with drinks. During the pandemic, I stressed about everything: Was it safe to go to the store? Get on a plane? Or meet with friends indoors or outside? The big thing I was looking for in a go-to recipe was **less** stress at the end of the day when I'm trying to get dinner together.

ENGLISH CREAM SCONES, PAGE 63

And because cooking fatigue is a real thing, even for me, I've also included lots of simply "assembled" dishes and boards in this book that don't even require you to turn on the stove. They really take my idea of "store-bought is just fine" to a new level, but you do need to search out really good components for them to be special. A traditional English ploughman's lunch inspired me to create a glorious board filled with lots of delicious things to eat—honey-baked ham, jammy eggs, a big slice of coarse pâté, aged sharp English Cheddar, sweet fig preserves, celery stalks, plus a big green salad and a basket of breads—none of them cooked by me, but artfully arranged and completely appealing. I'd be very happy to have that for dinner, wouldn't you? You can even apply this idea to dessert, assembling a board with store-bought fruit plus sweets from a bakery, as I have on page 245. And when my French Bistro Salad (page 102) and Heirloom Tomato & Blue Cheese Salad (page 105) come together with fresh farm-stand ingredients they're just fabulous, and there's no cooking at all!

All of these special qualities—Easy, Make Ahead, Prep Ahead, Freeze Ahead, or Assembled—are at the heart of my new list of Go-To Dinners, and you'll see these features noted throughout the book. I've even provided suggestions for using leftovers with notes on "two-fers" when appropriate, and I hope these will inspire you to come up with ideas of your own!

Above all else, though, a go-to recipe should be simple to follow and work every time. It must be easy to prepare and still delicious enough to get everyone to your table so you, too, can create a happy community of family and friends around yourself. We all need that in our lives and I think you'll agree that it all starts with dinner.

XXXX Ina

drinks & apps

Bourbon Arnold Palmers

Watermelon Cosmopolitans

Pink Grapefruit Palomas

Pomegranate Spritzers

Hot Spiced Mulled Wine

Smoked Salmon Quesadillas

Creamy Hummus

Easy Oysters Rockefeller

Goat Cheese Toasts

Chipotle Cheddar Crackers

Antipasto Board

go-to cocktails

When someone new is coming to dinner,

I pretty much always make the same "getting to know you" menu: the rack of lamb, orzo with roasted vegetables, and apple crostata from my second cookbook, *Barefoot Contessa Parties*. It's really delicious, I've made it so many times that I can almost do it with my eyes closed, and it allows me to pay more attention to my new guests than to cooking the meal. But the thing that really makes the party sparkle—especially with people I don't know very well—is the cocktail I serve when they walk in the door.

There's something about offering a guest a special drink that says, "We're having a party!" and "I'm happy to see you." I'm not sure if it's the clink of ice in the cocktail shaker or the martini glasses that makes everyone feel festive and glamorous but it really does the trick. Of course, the cocktail has to be delicious, too.

For years, I made real Whiskey Sours with good bourbon plus freshly squeezed lemon and lime juice. They're delicious and guests often tell me they remind them of a parent or grandparent. Lately I've updated my "getting to know you" cocktail to something a little more modern: Watermelon Cosmopolitans (page 26) made with puréed watermelon juice, freshly squeezed lime juice, Cointreau, and vodka served in ice-cold martini glasses with a big sprig of mint. Everyone loves them!

There are a few tricks to pulling off cocktails without stress. Most drink recipes make just one drink at a time but who wants to be in the kitchen making cocktails while friends are arriving for dinner? All of my drink recipes are made in a big pitcher so you can prepare them in batches ahead of time. And if you can find a really large cocktail shaker, it's so much more efficient for chilling lots of drinks at once. I also put the martini glasses in the freezer for about 30 minutes so they're frosty cold when I pour in the drinks. And to make sure the ice is fresh, I empty the ice maker every week or so and let it fill up overnight.

Now that I've updated my "getting to know you" cocktail, I'm thinking it's time to update the dinner too. How does Rosemary Roasted Pork Tenderloins (page 135) and Roasted Fingerling Potatoes & Almost Any Green Vegetable (page 185) with a Dark Chocolate Tart (page 215) for dessert sound? Just like the old menu, this one lets me get almost everything done in advance so I can spend my time getting to know new friends. Which is why we entertain in the first place, right?

Jennifer Naylor is an extraordinary caterer in LA. When I saw that she had made Bourbon Arnold Palmers with lemonade, iced tea, and bourbon for a party, I thought they sounded fantastic. You can even make a "virgin" pitcher without the alcohol to drink all day, then add the bourbon at 5 p.m.!

bourbon arnold palmers

2 tea bags, such as Earl Grey or English Breakfast

2 cups boiling water

½ cup freshly squeezed lemon juice (3 lemons)

½ cup simple syrup (see note)

1 cup good bourbon, such as Maker's Mark

½ lemon, halved through the stem and cut in ¼-inch-thick half-rounds

SERVES 6

Place the tea bags in a 2-cup glass measuring cup and add the boiling water. Steep for 10 minutes, then discard the tea bags.

Meanwhile, combine the lemon juice, simple syrup, bourbon, and 2 cups water in a glass pitcher. Stir in the brewed tea and refrigerate until cold.

To serve, fill glasses half full with ice and pour in the drink mixture. Garnish with a lemon slice and serve ice cold.

To make simple syrup, bring 1 cup sugar and 1 cup water to a boil in a small saucepan and cook until the sugar dissolves. Refrigerate until cold.

You can mix the drink early in the day and refrigerate it, but serve it the same day because fresh lemon juice changes flavor overnight.

EASY / MAKE AHEAD

My friends Rob Marshall and John DeLuca love creating new cocktails. Their delicious variation on a Cosmo has become my go-to summer drink because everyone loves this refreshing blend of watermelon purée spiked with a hit of fresh lime juice plus vodka. Yum! I serve it in frozen martini glasses.

watermelon cosmopolitans

4 cups (¾-inch) diced red watermelon (see note)

6 ounces good vodka, such as Grey Goose

3 ounces Cointreau or triple sec

2 ounces freshly squeezed lime juice (2 limes)

4 large mint sprigs, for garnish

MAKES 4 DRINKS

Place four martini glasses in the freezer to chill for at least 30 minutes.

Place a food mill fitted with the largest disk over a bowl. Add the watermelon and pass it through the mill; you should end up with about 2 cups of watermelon juice. Pour into a pitcher and discard the seeds and pulp. Stir in the vodka, Cointreau, and lime juice.

Fill a cocktail shaker half full with ice, pour in the cocktail mixture, and shake for a full 30 seconds. Pour into the chilled martini glasses and garnish each glass with a sprig of mint. Serve ice cold.

If you make this with seedless watermelon (or carefully deseed regular watermelon), you can purée the watermelon in a blender and pour it through a fine-mesh sieve to remove the pulp.

MAKE AHEAD

Palomas are traditionally served in a glass with a salted rim, as margaritas are, but I always thought that made the drink too salty. I tried a sugar rim but that was too sweet. Finally, I mixed salt and sugar and voilà! The perfect rim to complement a perfect summer cocktail.

pink grapefruit palomas

¼ cup kosher salt

2 tablespoons sugar

Grapefruit wedge, plus more for garnish

1 cup freshly squeezed pink or ruby grapefruit juice (1 to 2 grapefruits)

1 cup tequila blanco, such as Casamigos

¼ cup freshly squeezed lime juice (2 limes)

2 tablespoons simple syrup (see note, page 25)

SERVES 4

Combine the ¼ cup salt and the sugar on a small plate. Run a wedge of grapefruit around the rim of four (10-ounce) glasses to moisten. Lightly dip the rims in the sugar mixture and set aside to dry.

Meanwhile, combine the grapefruit juice, tequila, lime juice, simple syrup, and a pinch of salt in a pitcher and stir to blend. Fill a cocktail shaker half full with ice and pour in the cocktail mixture (you may have to do this in batches). Shake for a full 30 seconds to chill and slightly dilute the cocktail. Pour into two of the prepared glasses, add a few ice cubes and a wedge of grapefruit, and serve ice cold. Repeat with the remaining mixture and glasses.

EASY

It should be easy to make a good nonalcoholic cocktail but it's actually not. Without alcohol, a cocktail needs the tart bite of citrus or it feels like you're just drinking fruit punch. Blending pomegranate juice with freshly squeezed lime and serving it in a martini glass really delivers that sophisticated cocktail experience, even though it is zero proof.

pomegranate spritzers

2 cups chilled sparkling water, such as Pellegrino

2 tablespoons pomegranate juice, such as Pom Wonderful

2 tablespoons freshly squeezed lime juice (2 limes)

Fresh pomegranate seeds and lime slices, for serving

MAKES 4 DRINKS

Place four martini glasses in the freezer to chill for at least 30 minutes.

Pour the sparkling water, pomegranate juice, and lime juice into a large pitcher. Add some ice and stir for 30 seconds to chill the drink. Strain the mixture into the prepared martini glasses, add a few pomegranate seeds and a slice of lime to each glass and serve ice cold.

If you want to make a larger batch for a crowd, combine the sparkling water, pomegranate juice, and lime juice in a large pitcher and serve in highball glasses filled with ice. Garnish with pomegranate seeds and a slice of lime.

EASY

On a cold winter day, a hot drink is like curling up with a big cozy blanket. Hot spiced Cabernet wine with fresh apple cider has all the wintery flavors of a good apple pie—cinnamon, cloves, orange zest—plus the sweetness of a little honey. It will warm your insides.

hot spiced mulled wine

1 large navel orange

4 cups fresh apple cider

1 (750 ml) bottle spicy red wine, such as Cabernet Sauvignon

¼ cup liquid honey

2 (3-inch) cinnamon sticks

8 whole dried cloves

4 whole dried star anise

SERVES 8

With a sharp knife, remove the peel from the orange in 12 long strips, trying to get as little of the white pith as possible. Juice the orange directly into a large saucepan.

Add the apple cider, wine, honey, cinnamon sticks, cloves, and star anise to the pan along with 4 of the orange peel strips (reserve the rest for serving). Bring the mixture to a boil, lower the heat, and simmer for 10 minutes. Strain into heatproof glasses or mugs and garnish each drink with an orange peel. Serve hot.

MAKE AHEAD

Quesadillas are a great appetizer because you can assemble them in advance and fry them just before dinner. These small flour tortillas are filled with smoked salmon, cream cheese, Cheddar, and dill and served with sour cream.

smoked salmon quesadillas

6 ounces cream cheese, at room temperature

½ cup chopped scallions, white and green parts (2 scallions)

3 ounces thinly sliced smoked salmon, chopped

2 tablespoons minced fresh dill, plus extra for serving

3 ounces grated Monterey Jack or yellow Cheddar

Kosher salt and freshly ground black pepper

6 (8-inch) flour tortillas

¾ cup sour cream

1 teaspoon finely grated lime zest

8 tablespoons (1 stick) unsalted butter, melted

2 to 3 ounces salmon roe (optional)

SERVES 6

Place the cream cheese, scallions, salmon, dill, Monterey Jack, ½ teaspoon salt, and ¼ teaspoon pepper in a bowl and lightly mix with a fork.

Place three of the tortillas on a work surface and top each with the cheese-and-salmon mixture, spreading it evenly over the entire tortilla with a knife or offset spatula. Place the remaining tortillas on top and press lightly. Combine the sour cream and lime zest in a small bowl and set aside.

Brush the top of one tortilla completely with the melted butter. Heat a 10-inch sauté pan over medium heat and place the quesadilla, butter side down, in the sauté pan. Brush the top with butter. Cook for about 2 minutes, until golden brown and blistered. Carefully flip the quesadilla and cook for another 2 minutes. Remove to a cutting board. Repeat for the remaining quesadillas.

To serve, cut each quesadilla in 4 to 6 wedges with a big knife and serve warm with the sour cream and salmon roe, if using, on the side.

The quesadillas can be assembled ahead and refrigerated for a few hours. Fry them before serving.

PREP AHEAD

Sometimes it's just fun to update a classic. In my first cookbook, The Barefoot Contessa Cookbook, *I have a recipe for hummus that is chunky and delicious and very easy to make. This is a more refined version. The step of removing the chickpea skins may seem fussy, but the result is a luxuriously silky hummus. I serve this with whole chickpeas, Marcona almonds, and smoked paprika for flavor and crunch.*

creamy hummus

2 (15.5-ounce) cans chickpeas, rinsed and drained

½ teaspoon baking powder

⅓ cup freshly squeezed lemon juice, plus extra (3 lemons)

1 tablespoon garlic finely grated on a Microplane (4 cloves)

¼ teaspoon Tabasco sauce

¼ teaspoon smoked paprika, plus extra for garnish

Kosher salt and freshly ground black pepper

½ cup tahini (see note)

Good olive oil

¼ cup salted, roasted Marcona almonds, roughly chopped

Toasted pita triangles, for serving (see note)

SERVES 6

If the tahini has separated, purée it in a food processor fitted with the steel blade until smooth.

To toast the pita triangles, spread them on a sheet pan and bake at 350 degrees for 10 minutes.

MAKE AHEAD

Combine the chickpeas, baking powder, and 6 cups water in a large saucepan, cover, and bring to a boil over high heat. Uncover, lower the heat, and simmer for 25 minutes, stirring occasionally.

Meanwhile, combine the ⅓ cup lemon juice and the garlic in a small bowl and set aside.

Drain the water and any chickpea skins that have floated to the surface, leaving the chickpeas in the pan. Add cold water to cover, stir vigorously to loosen more skins, and again drain the water and skins that float to the top. Repeat 5 or 6 more times, until most of the skins are removed. Drain the chickpeas and place in the bowl of a food processor fitted with the steel blade, setting aside 2 tablespoons of whole chickpeas for the garnish. Add the lemon-and-garlic mixture, Tabasco, paprika, ¼ cup warm water, 1 tablespoon salt, and 1 teaspoon pepper. Process until very smooth, scraping down the bowl as needed. Add the tahini and 2 tablespoons olive oil and purée for one full minute, until creamy. Add 2 to 3 tablespoons of extra lemon juice to taste, 1 teaspoon salt, and enough warm water (1 tablespoon at a time) to make the hummus the consistency of yogurt. Taste for seasonings.

With a rubber spatula, spread the hummus on a large flat serving plate or shallow bowl, leaving a 2-inch border. Sprinkle with the reserved chickpeas and almonds. Drizzle with olive oil, sprinkle with paprika, and serve with toasted pita triangles.

The original recipe for Oysters Rockefeller was from the fabled New Orleans restaurant Antoine's. It was named after John D. Rockefeller because both he and the dish were so rich! Using frozen creamed spinach makes this one a snap to prepare.

easy oysters rockefeller

24 very fresh oysters on the half shell

4 tablespoons (½ stick) unsalted butter

½ cup finely chopped shallots (2 large)

¼ cup Pernod liqueur

Kosher salt and freshly ground black pepper

1 (9-ounce) package Seabrook frozen creamed spinach, defrosted (see note)

½ cup freshly grated Italian Parmesan cheese (2 ounces)

½ cup grated Gruyère cheese (2 ounces)

Fleur de sel or sea salt, for serving

MAKES 2 DOZEN OYSTERS / SERVES 6 TO 8

Preheat the oven to 450 degrees. Crinkle aluminum foil deeply and place on a sheet pan to hold the oyster shells level. Nestle the oysters into the foil in one layer, making sure not to spill any of their juices.

Melt the butter over medium heat in a small (8-inch) sauté pan. Add the shallots and sauté for 5 to 6 minutes, until tender and beginning to brown. Add the Pernod, 1 teaspoon kosher salt, and ½ teaspoon pepper and cook for 2 to 3 minutes to reduce the liquid. Stir in the spinach and cook for 2 minutes, until the liquid is absorbed. Taste for seasonings.

Spoon ½ tablespoon of the spinach mixture onto each oyster. Sprinkle the oysters evenly with the Parmesan and Gruyère. Bake for 6 to 8 minutes, until the spinach is hot and the cheese is melted. The oysters should be warm but not cooked through. Sprinkle with fleur de sel and serve hot.

If you can't find Seabrook frozen creamed spinach, you can use one (10-ounce) package of Green Giant frozen creamed spinach instead.

PREP AHEAD

Whenever I have leftover baguette, I slice it diagonally and keep it in the freezer so I can make these cheesy toasts in minutes. Toast the bread slices, then add the garlic and goat cheese. They're perfect to serve with drinks or as a crouton to float on top of a bowl of soup.

goat cheese toasts

1 fresh baguette

Good olive oil

Kosher salt and freshly ground black pepper

1 or 2 garlic cloves, halved lengthwise

8 ounces creamy goat cheese, such as Montrachet, at room temperature

Pitted green olives, such as Castelvetrano, halved

MAKES 12 TOASTS

Preheat the oven to 400 degrees.

Slice the baguette diagonally into twelve (¼-inch-thick) slices. Lay the slices in one layer on a sheet pan, brush each with olive oil, and sprinkle with salt and pepper. Bake the toasts for 8 to 10 minutes, until they are browned and crisp. As soon as they are cool enough to handle, rub one side of the toasts with the cut side of the garlic. Let cool, then spread the toasts with goat cheese and place the olives on top. Serve warm or at room temperature.

EASY

One of my go-to tricks is to keep some dough for slice-and-bake crackers in the freezer that I can throw in the oven when people are coming for drinks. The sharp Vermont Cheddar and spicy chipotle chili powder with crunchy sea salt really wake up everyone's taste buds. My friends can't stop eating these!

chipotle cheddar crackers

¼ pound (1 stick) unsalted butter, at room temperature

½ pound aged Cheddar, such as Grafton 2-year, grated (see note)

1 cup plus 2 tablespoons all-purpose flour

½ teaspoon ground chipotle powder

Kosher salt

Flaked sea salt, such as Maldon

MAKES 24 TO 28 CRACKERS

In the bowl of an electric mixer fitted with the paddle attachment, place the butter, Cheddar, all of the flour, the chipotle powder, and 1 teaspoon kosher salt. Add 1½ tablespoons water and mix on low speed to combine the ingredients. Turn the mixer to medium and beat for 30 seconds, until the ingredients come together in big clumps.

Transfer the dough to a lightly floured cutting board and roll it into a log 12 inches long by 1½ inches wide. Wrap in plastic and refrigerate for at least one hour. (You can refrigerate the dough for several days or freeze it for up to 4 months.)

When ready to bake, preheat the oven to 350 degrees.

Line two sheet pans with parchment paper. Slice the dough ½ inch thick (see note) and place the rounds 1 inch apart on the parchment paper. Sprinkle with sea salt and bake for 15 to 17 minutes, until golden brown. Cool on the sheet pans or a baking rack and serve at room temperature.

Grate the Cheddar on a box grater or in a food processor fitted with the carrot-grating disk.

I use a 3- to 4-inch paring knife, dipping it in warm water occasionally to make slicing easier.

FREEZE AHEAD

antipasto board

For a bite to serve with cocktails in the living room or as a first course at the table, an antipasto platter is so much more fun and colorful than putting little bowls of nibbles out. The options for an antipasto spread are incredibly varied, although I try to use mostly (maybe not all!) Italian components so everything goes together. Here are a few ideas to choose from:

Italian cheeses, such as

    Taleggio

    Mozzarella or bocconcini

    Fontina

    Truffled Pecorino

    Gorgonzola

Cured and sliced meats, such as

    Salami

    Prosciutto

    Coppa (dried capicola)

    Mortadella

Balsamic-Roasted Baby Peppers (page 176) or jarred peppers

Good olives, such as Castelvetrano

Cherry tomatoes

Whole-grain mustard

Breadsticks

ASSEMBLED

breakfast *for* dinner

Scrambled Eggs Cacio e Pepe

Roasted Vegetables with Jammy Eggs

Avocado & Fried Egg Tartines

Overnight Irish Oatmeal

English Cream Scones

Fresh Strawberry Rhubarb Preserves

Croissants with Smoked Salmon

Easy Eggs in Purgatory

Blueberry Ricotta Breakfast Cake

Vanilla Coffee Shakerato

Breakfast-for-Dinner Board

breakfast for dinner

Several years ago, I invited some friends for dinner and I really didn't have time to shop for and cook a traditional meal. Instead, I decided to go rogue and put together an impromptu breakfast buffet. I served Roasted Vegetables with Jammy Eggs (page 52) and big crisp strips of applewood smoked bacon, I toasted some whole-grain bread, and made a Blueberry Ricotta Breakfast Cake (page 71) for dessert. I had no idea what people would think about having breakfast for dinner—would they be delighted or disappointed?? Well, they were over the moon!! People who never took seconds were going back to the buffet with glee for more vegetables and ricotta cake. The whole meal was so unexpected and fun.

Since then, breakfast for dinner has become a bit of a tradition at my house, whether serving friends or just Jeffrey and me. I love breakfast food but who has time or energy to prepare a big meal in the morning? Breakfast is usually coffee and toast or a bowl of oatmeal while I read the paper and wake up; eating a big meal early in the day just makes me want to go right back to bed! As an evening meal, though, it's cozy and satisfying and when it's served with a delicious dessert, it really does feel like dinner.

Breakfast for dinner doesn't have to be a big stack of pancakes with butter and maple syrup. It can be more sophisticated, like Easy Eggs in Purgatory (page 68), eggs cooked in a rich tomato sauce, or Scrambled Eggs Cacio e Pepe (page 51) served with Slow-Roasted Tomatoes with Fennel (page 179). It can also be a little sweet and a little savory, like a warm croissant filled with smoked salmon and mascarpone, or soft-boiled eggs served with English Cream Scones (page 63) and homemade Fresh Strawberry Rhubarb Preserves (page 64).

Whether you're serving your family or a group of friends, everyone really loves breakfast for dinner. There is something a little naughty about it that just adds to the fun, and it takes so much less time to prepare than a traditional dinner, so even the cook is happy!

Eggs are always my go-to breakfast for dinner because they're substantial without being heavy, but I like to dress them up, like adding spicy Italian Pecorino cheese and pepper. You may even already have all the ingredients in the fridge! Just take your time with the cooking and you'll serve the most delicious scrambled eggs ever.

scrambled eggs cacio e pepe

12 extra-large eggs

1 cup whole milk

Kosher salt and freshly ground black pepper

4 tablespoons (½ stick) unsalted butter, quartered

⅔ cup freshly grated Italian Pecorino cheese, plus extra for serving

4 to 5 slices toasted country bread

SERVES 4 TO 5

Whisk the eggs, milk, and 2 teaspoons salt together in a medium bowl. Put the butter in a **cold** large (12-inch) sauté pan and place it over medium-low heat. Allow the butter to melt *almost* completely, then add the egg mixture. Cook over medium-low for 8 to 10 minutes, stirring occasionally with a rubber spatula. When the eggs start to make small clumps, stir them more rapidly, scraping the bottom of the pan, and cook for another 4 to 5 minutes. When the eggs are *almost* cooked, turn off the heat and continue to stir the eggs rapidly until they're soft and custardy. (When you pull the spatula through the eggs, they will still be soft but they will stay in place.) Stir in the Pecorino and 2 teaspoons pepper. Spoon the eggs over the toasted bread and serve hot sprinkled with extra Pecorino.

EASY

I loved Danny Meyer's NYC restaurant Maialino. When I went for Sunday brunch, I often ordered their roasted vegetables with eggs. You can prep everything ahead, roast the vegetables before dinner, then just add one or two eggs per person and serve. The sweet roasted vegetables are so good with the jammy soft-boiled eggs.

roasted vegetables with jammy eggs

2 cups (¾-inch) peeled and diced butternut squash (1 pound)

3 cups fingerling potatoes, halved or quartered (1 pound) (see note)

2 cups (¾-inch) peeled and diced celery root

2 cups (¾-inch) diced carrots, scrubbed (9 ounces)

3 large shallots, peeled, halved or quartered through the stem

Good olive oil

1 teaspoon minced fresh thyme leaves

Kosher salt and freshly ground black pepper

2 tablespoons Garlic & Herb Butter, diced (recipe follows)

4 cold extra-large eggs

Minced fresh chives or parsley

4 slices country bread, toasted

SERVES 4

Preheat the oven to 425 degrees.

Place the squash, potatoes, celery root, carrots, and shallots on a sheet pan, drizzle with ¼ cup olive oil, and sprinkle with the thyme, 2 teaspoons salt, and 1 teaspoon pepper. Toss with your hands to coat, then spread out in one layer. Roast for 40 to 45 minutes, until tender and starting to brown, tossing occasionally. Add the butter and roast for 5 more minutes. Toss the vegetables with the melted butter.

Meanwhile, fill a medium saucepan with water and bring to a boil. With a spoon, carefully lower each of the eggs into the boiling water and lower the heat until the water is at a low simmer. (You don't want the eggs knocking around in boiling water or they will crack.) Cook the eggs for 6½ minutes *exactly*, remove them from the saucepan, run them under cool water, and peel.

Divide the roasted vegetables among four dinner plates. Place one egg in the middle of each, cut it in half, and sprinkle with chives, salt, and pepper. Serve hot with a slice of toasted bread.

If you increase this recipe, use two sheet pans or the vegetables will steam instead of roasting.

If you can't find fingerling potatoes, use small Yukon Gold potatoes, halved or quartered.

Prep the vegetables and place them in a plastic storage bag with a damp paper towel to keep them moist and crisp. Refrigerate for up to a day.

PREP AHEAD / MAKE AHEAD

garlic & herb butter

½ pound (2 sticks) salted butter, at room temperature

2 tablespoons minced garlic (6 cloves)

½ cup minced fresh parsley

¼ cup minced fresh dill

¼ cup minced scallions, white and green parts (3 scallions)

1 teaspoon minced fresh rosemary

½ teaspoon grated lemon zest

1 tablespoon freshly squeezed lemon juice

Kosher salt and freshly ground black pepper

MAKES ¾ POUND

Place the butter in the bowl of an electric mixer fitted with the paddle attachment or use a hand mixer. Add the garlic, parsley, dill, scallions, rosemary, lemon zest, lemon juice, 1 tablespoon salt, and 1½ teaspoons pepper and mix on medium speed for 1 minute, until thoroughly combined.

Scrape the butter mixture onto one edge of a 12-inch-wide sheet of parchment paper and roll it up into a log 8 to 10 inches long and 1½ inches thick. Twist the ends of the paper to seal the log and refrigerate until firm. Refrigerate leftovers for up to a week or freeze for up to 4 months.

TWO-FER: *Serve sliced on grilled steak, chicken, or roasted vegetables.*

MAKE AHEAD / FREEZE AHEAD

For a quick and satisfying meal, I love tartines, which is what the French call open-faced sandwiches. These tartines have great flavor and they're a whole meal in a sandwich. I toast some bread, mash some avocados, roast a little prosciutto, and fry some eggs. Put them all together and I'm a happy camper.

avocado & fried egg tartines

4 ounces Italian prosciutto (4 to 8 slices)

4 large (½-inch-thick) slices rustic bread, such as sourdough

2 ripe Hass avocados, halved and pitted

2 tablespoons freshly squeezed lemon juice

½ teaspoon Sriracha

Kosher salt and freshly ground black pepper

2 tablespoons (¼ stick) unsalted butter

4 extra-large eggs

Microgreens or baby arugula

SERVES 2 TO 4

Preheat the oven to 375 degrees.

Place the prosciutto in one layer on a sheet pan lined with parchment paper. Roast for 7 to 9 minutes, until the prosciutto starts to brown. Set aside.

Meanwhile, on a second sheet pan, arrange the bread in one layer and toast in the oven for 12 to 15 minutes, turning once, until lightly browned. Scoop the avocados into a bowl and mash them roughly with a fork along with the lemon juice, Sriracha, 1 teaspoon salt, and ½ teaspoon pepper. Set aside.

Melt the butter in a large (12-inch) sauté pan over medium heat just until the foam subsides. Carefully crack the eggs into four opposite sides of the pan, sprinkle with salt and pepper, and cook for one minute, until the whites start to set. Lower the heat to medium-low, cover the pan (see note), and cook for 2 to 3 minutes, until the whites are completely set but the yolks are still runny.

Spread the toasts evenly with the avocado mixture, then place one egg on each toast. Top with the prosciutto and sprinkle with a few microgreens. Serve hot.

If you don't have the exact right lid for the pan, use a larger lid or even a sheet pan.

EASY

People always ask me what my ultimate comfort food is, expecting me to say something like mac & cheese or a burger and fries. But truthfully, when I'm cranky or tired, nothing makes me feel better than a delicious bowl of oatmeal—any time of the day. This salty and sweet version that you make ahead and reheat is crunchy and delicious.

overnight irish oatmeal

1½ cups steel-cut oats, such as McCann's

Kosher salt

Chopped salted nuts, such as almonds and cashews

Dried cranberries or raisins

Whole milk, for serving

Butter, brown sugar, and/or maple syrup, for serving

SERVES 6

Put 6 cups of water in a large saucepan and stir in the oats and 2 teaspoons salt. Bring to a boil over medium-high heat, lower the heat to simmer, and cook for exactly 2 minutes. Cover the pan and set aside at room temperature for 2 hours, then refrigerate overnight.

The next day, reheat the oatmeal and simmer uncovered for a few minutes, until hot. It should be creamy but still have some texture. (Add a little extra water if it's too thick.) Spoon the oatmeal into bowls and sprinkle with the nuts and cranberries. Serve hot with milk, butter, brown sugar, and/or maple syrup.

The oatmeal can stay in the fridge for up to a week. You can reheat one bowl at a time in a microwave, adding water, if necessary.

Be creative with the addition of fruits and nuts to make it different each time.

MAKE AHEAD

Cream tea is a particularly English form of afternoon tea that usually consists of scones, English cream, such as Devon cream, preserves, and sometimes butter. I find these scones so satisfying and, served warm from the oven with some scrambled eggs and homemade jam, they make breakfast for dinner really special.

english cream scones

4 cups plus 1 tablespoon all-purpose flour

2 tablespoons sugar, plus additional for sprinkling

2 tablespoons baking powder

Kosher salt

¾ pound (3 sticks) cold unsalted butter, ½-inch diced

4 extra-large eggs

1 cup cold heavy cream

¾ cup dried currants

1 egg beaten with 2 tablespoons water or milk, for egg wash

Clotted or Devon cream and Fresh Strawberry Rhubarb Preserves (page 64), for serving

MAKES 14 TO 16 LARGE SCONES

Preheat the oven to 400 degrees. Line two sheet pans with parchment paper.

In the bowl of an electric mixer fitted with the paddle attachment, combine the 4 cups of flour, 2 tablespoons sugar, baking powder, and 4 teaspoons salt. Add the butter and mix on the lowest speed until the butter is the size of peas. Whisk together the eggs and heavy cream and, with the mixer on low, quickly add them to the flour-and-butter mixture, combining just until blended. Toss the currants with the remaining 1 tablespoon flour, add them to the dough, and mix quickly to distribute the currants. The dough may be quite sticky.

Dump the dough onto a well-floured surface and knead a few times to be sure the ingredients are combined. You should still see lumps of butter in the dough. With floured hands, pat the dough into a circle, then use a floured rolling pin to roll the dough ¾ inch thick. Cut with a 3-inch plain round cutter and place the scones on the prepared sheet pans.

Brush the tops of the dough with the egg wash. Sprinkle with sugar and bake for 20 to 25 minutes, until the tops are browned and the insides feel firm when you press on the top. Serve warm with clotted cream and preserves.

Cut out the dough, wrap in plastic, and refrigerate for up to 2 days or freeze for up to 4 months. Defrost overnight in the fridge before baking.

PREP AHEAD / FREEZE AHEAD / MAKE AHEAD

Strawberries and rhubarb are in season for such a short time and when they are, I'm compelled to make these preserves. One Granny Smith apple adds enough natural pectin to set the jam. The orange and Grand Marnier make this even better.

fresh strawberry rhubarb preserves

2 pounds fresh strawberries, hulled and halved or quartered

4 cups (¾-inch) diced fresh rhubarb (1 pound)

1 Granny Smith apple, peeled and grated

6 cups sugar

¼ cup Grand Marnier

Zest of 2 oranges

MAKES 6 CUPS

Place the strawberries, rhubarb, apple, sugar, Grand Marnier, orange zest, and ¼ cup of water in a medium (11-inch) heavy pot, such as Le Creuset, and toss well. Cover and bring to a boil over medium-low heat, stirring occasionally. Uncover and cook at a low boil for 25 to 30 minutes, until the mixture registers 220 degrees on a candy thermometer. Occasionally, skim and discard any foam that rises to the top.

To test the consistency of the preserves, spoon some onto a plate and place it in the freezer for 5 to 10 minutes. You want it to be slightly runny but not thick like preserves from a jar. If it does not jell, continue cooking for another few minutes and test again. Allow the mixture to cool in the pot to room temperature. Transfer the preserves to a covered container and refrigerate for up to 2 weeks or freeze for up to 4 months.

MAKE AHEAD / FREEZE AHEAD

One of my favorite restaurants in New York City is La Mercerie in Soho. Chef Marie-Aude Rose's food is country French and served elegantly. Her croissant with smoked salmon and mascarpone cheese is like a bagel and lox that took a trip to Paris. It's an easy breakfast-for-dinner because other than reheating the croissant (which doesn't count as cooking), this is just assembled!

croissants with smoked salmon

4 large fresh croissants

8.8 ounces Italian mascarpone (about 1 cup)

1½ tablespoons whole milk

1½ tablespoons minced fresh chives

Kosher salt and freshly ground black pepper

1½ tablespoons capers in brine, drained

½ pound thinly sliced smoked salmon, preferably Scottish

Very thinly sliced red onion (optional)

3 cups baby arugula (2 to 3 ounces)

SERVES 4

Preheat the oven to 350 degrees.

Place the croissants on a sheet pan lined with parchment paper. Bake for 8 minutes, until heated through. Set aside for 5 minutes to cool slightly.

Meanwhile, in a medium bowl, combine the mascarpone, milk, chives, 1 teaspoon salt, and ½ teaspoon pepper.

Slice each croissant in half horizontally with a serrated knife. Spread the bottom halves with the mascarpone mixture, then sprinkle evenly with the capers and lay the salmon evenly on top. Place a few slices of red onion on top, if using. Top with a generous handful of arugula and replace the tops of the croissants, browned side up. Serve while the croissants are still slightly warm.

ASSEMBLED

Missy Robbins has two amazing restaurants in Brooklyn—Lilia and Misi—and she's also written two wonderful cookbooks. This dish was inspired by one of her recipes but instead of making arrabbiata sauce from scratch, I use Rao's jarred arrabbiata. Heat the sauce in a sauté pan, add some eggs, then bake it until the eggs are barely cooked. With big chunks of toasted bread, dinner's ready!

easy eggs in purgatory

Good olive oil

1 cup thinly sliced yellow onions

1 garlic clove, minced

1 (24-ounce) jar Rao's Arrabbiata Sauce

⅛ teaspoon crushed red pepper flakes

1 (6-inch) sprig fresh rosemary

4 extra-large eggs

1 tablespoon freshly grated Italian Pecorino cheese

1½ teaspoons minced fresh parsley

Flaked sea salt, such as Maldon, and freshly ground black pepper

2 to 4 slices toasted country bread, for serving

SERVES 2

Heat 1 tablespoon of olive oil in a medium (10-inch) sauté pan. Add the onions and cook over medium to medium-low heat for 5 to 7 minutes, stirring occasionally, until tender and starting to brown. Add the garlic and cook for one minute. Add the arrabbiata sauce, red pepper flakes, and rosemary, bring to a simmer, and cook over medium-low heat for 5 minutes. Remove and discard the sprig of rosemary.

Carefully crack one of the eggs into a small (4-inch) bowl and gently slide it into one corner of the pan (don't break the yolk), using the edge of the bowl to make a slight indentation in the sauce as you pour the egg in. Repeat with the remaining 3 eggs, placing them on opposite sides of the pan. Cover the pan tightly and cook over medium-low heat for 4 to 6 minutes, until the egg whites are set but the yolks are still runny. Sprinkle with the Pecorino, parsley, sea salt, and black pepper, cover the pan again, and cook for one more minute.

To serve, use a large spoon to scoop up two eggs per person along with some of the sauce and carefully transfer to shallow bowls. Spoon the remaining sauce around the eggs and serve hot with the toasted bread.

EASY

Everyone who makes this cake can't believe how easy it is! The ricotta and sour cream keep the cake moist and the blueberries and lemon zest give it lots of flavor. Even if you're having breakfast for dinner, you still need to have dessert, right?

blueberry ricotta breakfast cake

10 tablespoons (1¼ sticks) unsalted butter, at room temperature

1 cup granulated sugar

3 extra-large eggs, at room temperature

1 cup whole-milk ricotta

2 tablespoons sour cream

1 teaspoon pure vanilla extract, such as Nielsen-Massey

1 teaspoon grated lemon zest

1¼ cups all-purpose flour

1 tablespoon baking powder

Kosher salt

2 cups fresh blueberries (12 ounces), divided

Sifted confectioners' sugar, for dusting

SERVES 8

Preheat the oven to 350 degrees. Grease and flour a 9-inch round springform pan, shaking out any excess flour.

Place the butter and sugar in the bowl of an electric mixer fitted with the paddle attachment and beat on medium speed for 3 minutes, until light and fluffy, scraping down the sides of the bowl as needed. With the mixer on low, add the eggs one at a time, mixing well after each addition. Add the ricotta, sour cream, vanilla, and lemon zest and mix well. (The batter will look curdled.)

In a small bowl, stir together the flour, baking powder, and 1 teaspoon salt. With the mixer on low, slowly add the dry ingredients to the batter, mixing just until incorporated. With a rubber spatula, fold two thirds of the blueberries into the batter. Transfer the batter to the prepared springform pan and smooth the top. Scatter the remaining blueberries on the cake, pressing them lightly into the surface.

Bake for 45 to 55 minutes, until a toothpick inserted in the center comes out clean. Transfer to a wire rack and allow to cool in the pan for 15 minutes. Remove the sides of the pan and *lightly* dust the top with the confectioners' sugar. Serve warm or at room temperature.

EASY / MAKE AHEAD

This drink was inspired by a recipe I saw in Bon Appétit *magazine. When I'm serving it for dinner, I make it with decaf coffee so I'm not up all night. I love the balance of coffee, sugar, and a hint of vanilla.*

vanilla coffee shakerato

¾ cup espresso or strong coffee (regular or decaf) (see note)

2 tablespoons sweetened condensed milk

1 tablespoon simple syrup (see note, page 25)

½ teaspoon pure vanilla extract

1½ cups ice cubes

MAKES 2 DRINKS

In a large cocktail shaker, stir together the espresso, condensed milk, simple syrup, and vanilla. Add the ice and shake for a full 30 seconds, until frothy and very cold. Pour the drink *and* the ice into two 8-ounce glasses and serve ice cold.

I use the "long" rather than "short" setting on my espresso machine. You can certainly make this with strong coffee as well.

EASY

breakfast-for-dinner board

A breakfast-for-dinner board can be anything you might want to eat for a special breakfast but all arranged beautifully on a round or rectangular board. This list is mostly things that you can assemble from a bakery and grocery store, but they look so much more beautiful served all together. Everyone will love having a buffet of delicious treats to choose from!

Ripe melon slices

Strawberries

Grapes

Fresh peaches

Mixed berries

Granola

Yogurt

Honey

Banana bread, sliced

Croissants

Scones

Whole-grain bread, sliced

Sliced ham or prosciutto

Jammy eggs (see page 52)

Fruit preserves

Good salted butter

Cream cheese

Muffins

ASSEMBLED

light dinners

Ravioli en Brodo

Creamy Potato Fennel Soup

Chicken Ramen-Noodle Soup

Gruyère Omelet

Tuscan White Bean Soup

Lobster & Avocado Sandwiches

Hot Dogs in Puff Pastry

Winter Greens with Stilton & Hazelnuts

Warm Vegetable & Grain Bowl

Greek Orzo Salad

French Bistro Salad

Heirloom Tomato & Blue Cheese Salad

Caramelized Butternut Squash
with Burrata

Creamy Eggs with Lobster & Crab

Roasted Shrimp Panzanella

Provençal Orange Salad

Potato Salad à la Julia Child

Melon & Prosciutto

Ploughman's Lunch

learn something new!

My friend Jennifer Garner said something that has really stayed with me. As children, we're always learning new skills and we perfect them through lots of repetition. We snap on a pair of skis, careen down a mountain, and eventually we learn how to ski, no matter how many times we fall. In my twenties I taught myself to windsail. I spent way more time in the drink than I did standing on that board, but I tried over and over again until I got it right. As we get older, we're more reluctant to go through that embarrassing process because we're not comfortable failing. But avoiding failure means we miss out on the thrill of accomplishing something new.

The same is true in the kitchen. One of my best go-to light dinners is a simple Gruyère Omelet (page 88), an uncomplicated dish but one that takes some practice to make properly. Don't let that intimidate you though! Omelets are a staple in my house for several reasons. First, I always have the ingredients on hand: eggs, butter, cheese, salt, and pepper. Second, they literally take three minutes to make. And finally, they can be filled with anything from a sprinkling of cheese to whatever is left over from last night's dinner, like roasted vegetables or shredded chicken. (A friend's father even used to fill omelets with leftover Chinese food!)

The two most important tricks to making a perfect omelet are using the right-size nonstick pan and perfecting the flipping motion so the omelet ends up in the right shape—and all of it on the plate, not all over your stovetop. Just like learning a new sport, you may need to try this over and over again until you master the process (luckily even the test omelets will still taste good!). But once you've nailed the technique, an omelet will be one of your go-to dinners forever, an accomplishment well worth investing the effort!

Every country has its own chicken soup and this one is classic Italian. The key to its flavor is rich homemade chicken stock plus lots of vegetables, good ravioli, and a final sprinkling of Parmesan and fresh dill. The Parmesan rind and a squeeze of lemon at the end brighten all the flavors.

ravioli en brodo

Good olive oil

2 cups chopped yellow onions (2 onions)

2 cups (½-inch-thick) diagonally sliced carrots, scrubbed (3 to 5 carrots) (see note)

1½ cups (½-inch) diced celery (3 ribs)

1½ cups (½-inch) diced fennel, top and core removed

8 cups simmering chicken stock, preferably homemade (recipe follows)

1 Italian Parmesan cheese rind (about 2 × 3 inches)

Kosher salt and freshly ground black pepper

1 pound cheese ravioli, fresh or frozen

Freshly grated Italian Parmesan cheese, for serving

Minced fresh dill or parsley, for serving

Freshly squeezed lemon juice, for serving

SERVES 4 TO 6

Heat ¼ cup of olive oil in a medium (10 to 11-inch) pot or Dutch oven, such as Le Creuset, over medium heat. Add the onions, carrots, celery, and fennel and sauté for 10 to 15 minutes, stirring occasionally, until the vegetables are softened. Add the chicken stock, 2 cups water, the Parmesan rind, 1 tablespoon salt, and 1 teaspoon pepper. Bring to a boil, lower the heat, and simmer, partially covered, for 20 minutes, stirring occasionally. Remove the Parmesan rind and taste the soup for seasonings.

Meanwhile, cook the ravioli in a large pot of boiling water with 2 tablespoons salt for 4 to 6 minutes (or according to the directions on the package), stirring occasionally. Drain and spread out on a plate so they don't stick together.

For serving, place the warm ravioli in large soup bowls and ladle the hot soup over them. Sprinkle with Parmesan, dill, and a squeeze of lemon and serve hot.

Cut thick carrots in half lengthwise, then cut them ½ inch thick diagonally.

Prepare the soup without the ravioli and refrigerate for 5 days or freeze for up to 6 months. Before serving, cook the ravioli and serve with the soup.

MAKE AHEAD

I think of homemade chicken stock as liquid gold. Nothing available on the market has the depth of flavor or richness of stock you've made yourself. It contributes such great body and aroma to so many dishes. Plus, having a big pot of chicken stock simmering away on my stove just makes me feel good.

homemade chicken stock

3 (5-pound) roasting chickens

3 large yellow onions, unpeeled and quartered

6 carrots, unpeeled and halved

4 celery stalks with leaves, cut into thirds

4 parsnips, unpeeled and halved

20 sprigs fresh parsley

15 sprigs fresh thyme

20 sprigs fresh dill

1 head garlic, unpeeled and cut in half crosswise

2 tablespoons kosher salt

2 teaspoons whole black peppercorns

MAKES 6 QUARTS

Place the chickens, onions, carrots, celery, parsnips, parsley, thyme, dill, garlic, salt, and peppercorns in a 16 to 20-quart stockpot. Add 7 quarts of water and bring to a boil. Lower the heat and simmer uncovered for 4 hours. Allow the stock to cool for 30 minutes. Strain the contents of the pot through a colander into a large bowl and discard the solids. Pack the stock in containers and refrigerate for up to a few days or freeze for up to 6 months.

FREEZE AHEAD

Puréed potato soup can be very satisfying but it can also be a little boring. I like to start with Yukon Gold potatoes, which are creamier than russets, then add lots of sautéed fennel, onions, and good chicken stock. A splash of Pernod at the end enhances the anise flavor of the fennel.

creamy potato fennel soup

Good olive oil

2 tablespoons (¼ stick) unsalted butter

5 cups sliced fennel, tops and cores removed (2 bulbs), fronds reserved

4 cups sliced yellow onions (3 onions)

1½ pounds Yukon Gold potatoes, peeled, 1-inch diced

5 cups good chicken stock, preferably homemade (page 83)

Kosher salt and freshly ground black pepper

2 tablespoons Pernod liqueur

1 cup half-and-half

Garnishes for serving, such as Meredith Dairy cheese, cubed creamy goat cheese, croutons, cooked crumbled bacon, and/or cooked pancetta

SERVES 6

Heat 3 tablespoons of olive oil and the butter in a medium (11-inch) pot or Dutch oven, such as Le Creuset, over medium-low heat. Add the fennel and onions and sauté for 15 minutes, stirring occasionally, until they begin to brown.

Add the potatoes, chicken stock, 1 tablespoon salt, and 1 teaspoon pepper and bring to a boil. Lower the heat, cover, and simmer for 30 minutes, until the potatoes are very tender.

In batches, purée the soup in a food processor fitted with the steel blade until smooth. Pour the soup back into the pot, stir in the Pernod and half-and-half, and taste for seasonings. Reheat over medium-low heat.

Place the garnishes in the middle of large, shallow soup bowls and pour the hot soup around them. Drizzle with olive oil, garnish with the reserved fennel fronds, and serve hot.

MAKE AHEAD / FREEZE AHEAD

When the pandemic started, we all stocked our pantries because we never knew when we'd be able to get to a grocery store. I bought some ramen noodles on one of those shopping trips and one day I discovered they make an easy and delicious addition to chicken soup. I added baby bok choy and ginger for flavor and texture.

chicken ramen-noodle soup

2 split (1 whole) chicken breasts, skin-on, bone-in

3 tablespoons canola or vegetable oil, plus extra for the chicken

Kosher salt and freshly ground black pepper

1½ cups chopped yellow onion (1 large)

2 cups (½-inch-thick) sliced carrots, scrubbed (3 to 5 carrots)

3 tablespoons peeled and minced fresh ginger

1 tablespoon minced garlic (3 cloves)

10 cups simmering chicken stock, preferably homemade (page 83)

1 tablespoon soy sauce, such as Kikkoman

1 (3-ounce) package ramen noodles (discard the flavor pack)

8 ounces baby bok choy, leaves separated, trimmed, and cleaned

6 scallions, white and green parts, trimmed and sliced diagonally

SERVES 6

Preheat the oven to 350 degrees. Place the chicken on a sheet pan, skin side up, rub with oil, sprinkle with salt and pepper, and roast for 30 to 40 minutes, until cooked through. Cool slightly, discard the skin and bones, and shred the meat in large pieces.

Meanwhile, heat the oil in a medium (10-inch) heavy-bottomed pot or Dutch oven, such as Le Creuset, over medium-low heat. Add the onion and sauté for 6 to 8 minutes, until tender. Add the carrots and sauté for 5 minutes. Add the ginger and garlic and sauté for one minute. Add the chicken stock, bring to a boil, lower the heat, and simmer for 10 minutes.

Add the shredded chicken to the stock and bring to a simmer. Add the soy sauce and taste for seasonings. Add the noodles. Cut the bok choy in ½-inch-thick diagonal slices and add *just* the stems to the soup, simmering for 2 to 3 minutes, until the noodles and bok choy are tender. Off the heat, stir in the bok choy leaves and scallions and serve hot.

To prep ahead or to freeze, make the soup up to adding the noodles, bok choy, and scallions. Reheat the soup, add the last 3 ingredients, and serve hot.

TWO-FER: *Instead of cooking the chicken breasts, you can add shredded leftover roast chicken (page 128).*

EASY

An omelet is the ultimate go-to dinner. It takes 30 seconds to prep and about two minutes to cook. It can be filled with whatever is in the fridge, from ham to roasted vegetables, but my favorite is this simple Gruyère omelet. It takes a few tries to get the technique down but then you're good for life.

gruyère omelet

3 extra-large eggs

Kosher salt and freshly ground black pepper

1 tablespoon salted or unsalted butter

¼ cup grated Gruyère or Cheddar cheese

SERVES 1

Be sure all your ingredients, particularly the grated cheese, are prepped before you start. Place the eggs, ½ teaspoon of salt, and a few grinds of pepper in a medium bowl and beat them with a fork for 20 to 30 seconds, until the whites and yolks are combined.

Put the butter in a cold nonstick 9-inch omelet pan (see note) and place the pan over medium-high heat to just melt the butter, tilting the pan so the butter covers the bottom of the pan.

Pour the egg mixture into the pan all at once, allowing the eggs to cook for 30 seconds, until there is a cooked layer on the bottom. Grabbing the handle with both hands, quickly push the pan away, then jerk it back toward you, forcing some of the eggs to roll over themselves on the far side of the pan. Sprinkle the Gruyère down the middle of the uncooked eggs and jerk the pan again, forcing the eggs to again fold over themselves (and the cheese) at the far side. Keep cooking and jerking the pan every 10 seconds and folding the omelet at the far side until the eggs are almost (but not totally) cooked. Allow the omelet to cook without moving for 5 seconds. Slide the omelet onto a plate, sprinkle with salt, and serve hot.

All-Clad makes a perfect 9-inch nonstick omelet pan.

REALLY FAST

Soup for dinner has to be really hearty, with lots of flavor and texture. This one starts with sautéed pancetta, leeks, onions, carrots, and celery. Then I add lots of rosemary, garlic, chicken stock, and white beans and let it simmer away. Soaking dried beans ahead may take some planning, but the result is a much richer, silkier soup.

tuscan white bean soup

1 pound dried white cannellini beans

Good olive oil

4 ounces pancetta, ¼-inch diced (see note)

2 cups chopped leeks, white and light green parts (2 leeks)

2 cups chopped yellow onions (2 onions)

2 cups (½-inch) diced carrots, scrubbed (3 to 5 carrots)

2 cups (½-inch) diced celery (4 ribs)

2 tablespoons minced garlic (6 cloves)

2 teaspoons minced fresh rosemary

8 to 10 cups good chicken stock, preferably homemade (page 83)

2 bay leaves

Kosher salt and freshly ground black pepper

Freshly grated Italian Parmesan cheese, for serving

MAKES 3 QUARTS / SERVES 6

Place the beans in a large bowl and add enough cold water to cover them by 2 inches. Refrigerate for at least 8 hours or overnight. Drain the beans, rinse under cold running water, and drain again. Set aside.

In a medium (10-inch) pot or Dutch oven, such as Le Creuset, heat ¼ cup of olive oil over medium heat. Add the pancetta and sauté for 4 to 5 minutes, until browned. Add the leeks, onions, carrots, celery, garlic, and rosemary and cook over medium-low for 10 minutes, stirring occasionally, until the vegetables are tender.

Add the beans, chicken stock, bay leaves, 1 tablespoon salt, and 1 teaspoon pepper to the pot and bring to a boil. Lower the heat and simmer, partially covered, for 1 hour and 30 minutes, until the beans are very tender. Stir occasionally, scraping the bottom of the pot, to prevent it from burning. Discard the bay leaves, cover the pot, and allow the soup to sit off the heat for 15 minutes.

Reheat, if necessary. Ladle into large shallow soup bowls, sprinkle with Parmesan cheese, drizzle with olive oil, and serve hot.

The soup will thicken as it stands. Reheat gently over medium heat, adding water as needed to achieve your preferred consistency.

You can sometimes find packages of pre-diced pancetta in the deli case near the bacon.

MAKE AHEAD / FREEZE AHEAD

Very few sandwiches feel special enough for dinner but I had some cooked lobster and I prepared a great high/low dinner, turning a humble avocado sandwich into something really special. Creamy avocado is perfect with the lemony lobster salad and crunchy celery. And, of course, everything tastes better on a potato roll!

lobster & avocado sandwiches

1 pound cooked lobster meat, medium-diced

1 cup (small-diced) celery (3 ribs)

¾ cup good mayonnaise, such as Hellmann's or Best

2½ tablespoons freshly squeezed lemon juice, divided

Kosher salt and freshly ground black pepper

3 ripe avocados, halved, pitted, and peeled

6 Martin's Sandwich Potato Rolls, lightly toasted (see note)

MAKES 6 SANDWICHES

Combine the lobster, celery, mayonnaise, 1 tablespoon of the lemon juice, 1 teaspoon salt, and ½ teaspoon pepper in a medium bowl and set aside.

Combine the avocados in another bowl with the remaining 1½ tablespoons of lemon juice, 1½ teaspoons salt, and ¾ teaspoon pepper and coarsely mash together with a fork.

Place the bottom halves of the rolls on a board and spread with the avocado mixture. Arrange the lobster mixture on top. Replace the roll tops and serve at room temperature.

To toast the rolls, I place them, cut sides down, on top of the toaster (not in the toaster) and turn the toaster on until they are nicely browned.

ASSEMBLED

If you prefer to cook the lobster yourself, two (2-pound) cooked lobsters will yield 1 pound of cooked lobster meat.

During the pandemic, I challenged myself to make something from ingredients I had on hand and post it on Instagram to give people ideas for dinner. One day, I had hot dogs, mustard, and frozen puff pastry and while they're just fancy pigs in blankets, I have to admit, they were pretty delicious!

hot dogs in puff pastry

All-purpose flour

2 sheets frozen puff pastry, thawed in the refrigerator

4 teaspoons Dijon mustard, such as Grey Poupon, divided

4 all-beef hot dogs, such as Hebrew National

1 egg beaten with 1 tablespoon water, for egg wash

Flaked sea salt, such as Maldon, and freshly ground black pepper

SERVES 2 TO 4

Preheat the oven to 375 degrees. Line a sheet pan with parchment paper.

Dust a cutting board lightly with flour and unfold one sheet of the pastry on the board. Roll lightly with a floured rolling pin to smooth out the folds. Cut two (5½ × 4-inch) rectangles of pastry. With the 5½-inch side facing you, brush 1 teaspoon of mustard across the lower half of each rectangle. Place a hot dog on top of the mustard toward the lower edge and roll the pastry up and away from you over the hot dog. The hot dog should be totally encased in pastry. Brush the far inside edge with the egg wash to seal the pastry and place it on the prepared sheet pan, seam side down. Repeat with the remaining puff pastry and hot dogs to make four rolls total.

Brush the tops and sides of puff pastry with the egg wash and sprinkle generously with the sea salt and pepper. Bake for 25 to 35 minutes, until the pastry is browned and cooked through. Serve hot with extra mustard on the side.

You can prep the rolls a few hours ahead and refrigerate them covered until ready to bake just before dinner.

EASY / PREP AHEAD

When I create a new recipe, I'm looking for flavor, color, and texture. This salad has all that and more—crisp, slightly bitter endive and radicchio, crunchy, fragrant hazelnuts, creamy sharp blue cheese, and a citrusy lemon vinaigrette. It all works so well together, and you don't even need to turn on the stove. I'm happy having this for dinner on its own, but you can always add a rotisserie chicken or grilled salmon.

winter greens with stilton & hazelnuts

2 small Belgian endives (½ pound)

1 small head Treviso or radicchio (½ pound)

1 head butter lettuce, washed and spun dry

3 ounces baby arugula

½ cup whole hazelnuts

½ pound English Stilton, coarsely crumbled

¼ cup freshly squeezed lemon juice (2 lemons)

½ cup good olive oil

¼ teaspoon Dijon mustard

Kosher salt and freshly ground black pepper

SERVES 4

Separate the leaves of the endive and Treviso and, if large, cut each leaf in half lengthwise. Place them in a large, low serving bowl. Tear the butter lettuce in large pieces and add to the bowl along with the arugula.

Place the hazelnuts in a small (8-inch) dry sauté pan and toast over low heat for 5 to 10 minutes, tossing often, until they become fragrant. Transfer the hazelnuts to a kitchen towel and rub as much of the skins off as possible. Chop the nuts coarsely. Add the nuts and Stilton to the salad.

In a 1-cup glass measuring cup, whisk together the lemon juice, olive oil, mustard, 1½ teaspoons salt, and ¾ teaspoon pepper. Pour just enough dressing over the salad to moisten and sprinkle with salt and pepper. Toss carefully and serve.

EASY

Le Pain Quotidien is a chain of wonderful cafés that originated in Belgium, and a lunch I had there inspired this hearty grain bowl. It's got so many great flavors and textures from earthy bulgur, roasted butternut squash, arugula, dried cranberries, toasted walnuts, and creamy goat cheese. Of course, if you want this heartier, you can always add some soft-boiled eggs or shredded chicken.

warm vegetable & grain bowl

¾ cup whole-grain bulgur wheat (5 ounces)

Kosher salt and freshly ground black pepper

½ red onion, cut into 8 wedges through the stem

1½ pounds butternut squash, ½-inch diced

½ pound heirloom baby carrots, scrubbed and halved lengthwise

1 tablespoon plus ½ cup good olive oil, divided

3 ounces baby arugula

4 ounces baby kale, julienned crosswise

½ cup frozen shelled edamame, defrosted

½ cup dried cranberries (2 ounces)

½ cup toasted walnuts or pecans (1½ ounces)

¼ cup Champagne or white wine vinegar

2 teaspoons Dijon mustard

½ teaspoon minced garlic

3 ounces creamy goat cheese, thickly sliced

SERVES 4

Preheat the oven to 400 degrees.

In a small saucepan, bring 1 cup of water to a boil. Remove from the heat, add the bulgur and 1 teaspoon salt, cover, and set aside for 30 minutes.

Meanwhile, combine the onion, butternut squash, and carrots on a sheet pan. Drizzle with the 1 tablespoon olive oil, sprinkle with 2 teaspoons salt and 1 teaspoon pepper, and toss well. Spread the vegetables in one layer and roast for 25 to 30 minutes, tossing once, until all the vegetables are tender.

Meanwhile, combine the arugula, kale, edamame, cranberries, and walnuts in a large bowl. In a small bowl, whisk together the vinegar, mustard, and garlic and slowly whisk in the ½ cup olive oil. While the bulgur and vegetables are still hot, pour enough vinaigrette on the greens to moisten and divide among four large bowls. Spoon a quarter of the bulgur and some goat cheese in the center of each bowl and distribute a quarter of the vegetables on top. Sprinkle with salt, drizzle with the extra vinaigrette, and serve warm.

PREP AHEAD

Round Swamp Farm is a third-generation family farm in East Hampton. Their prepared food and baked goods are simply outstanding. This recipe was inspired by one of their salads; it has all the Greek ingredients that I love—orzo, olives, feta, lemon, and dill.

greek orzo salad

1 cup orzo (about 8 ounces)

Kosher salt and freshly ground black pepper

¼ cup freshly squeezed lemon juice, plus extra for serving (2 lemons)

½ cup good olive oil

1 cup canned chickpeas, rinsed and drained

½ cup (¼-inch) diced red Holland bell pepper

½ cup (¼-inch) diced red onion

3 tablespoons capers in brine, drained

3 tablespoons minced fresh dill

4 ounces Greek feta, ½-inch diced (not crumbled)

½ cup Kalamata olives, pitted and halved lengthwise (see note)

2 cups baby arugula

½ lemon, thinly sliced, for serving

SERVES 6

Bring 6 cups of water to a boil in a large saucepan and add the orzo and 1 tablespoon salt. Return the water to a boil, lower the heat, and simmer for 8 to 10 minutes, until the orzo is al dente. Drain and transfer to a large bowl.

Meanwhile, whisk together the lemon juice, olive oil, 2 teaspoons salt, and 1 teaspoon black pepper in a 1-cup glass measuring cup. Pour the vinaigrette over the warm pasta and stir well. Add the chickpeas, bell pepper, onion, capers, dill, feta, and olives and combine carefully.

Just before serving, stir in the arugula, add some sliced lemon, a squeeze of lemon juice, and taste for seasonings. Serve warm or at room temperature.

If you can't find pitted Kalamata olives, you can buy unpitted ones and use a cherry pitter to remove the pits.

MAKE AHEAD

This classic French salad, inspired by one I had at Le Bilboquet in NYC, is so good that I could make a whole meal out of it. It's also easy to prep ahead, including the dressing, so you can just assemble it and serve either on its own or with some leftover roast chicken (page 128). The caramelized walnuts really make this special.

french bistro salad

1 large head radicchio (¾ pound)

2 Belgian endives (¾ pound)

2 Granny Smith apples, unpeeled

1 pound Roquefort cheese, thickly sliced, then crumbled

2 cups caramelized walnuts or pecans (7 ounces)

FOR THE VINAIGRETTE:

¼ cup good Champagne or white wine vinegar

3 tablespoons Dijon mustard, such as Grey Poupon

Kosher salt and freshly ground black pepper

½ cup good olive oil

SERVES 6

Cut the radicchio in half through the stem and remove the core. Place each half cut side down on a cutting board and thinly slice crosswise as you would cut for slaw. Place in a large bowl. Cut the endive in half through the core, remove the cores, and place each half cut side down on the cutting board. Thinly slice the endive at a 45-degree angle to make long shreds and add to the radicchio. With a knife or a mandoline set to the thinnest julienne setting, cut each apple in matchsticks and add to the bowl.

For the vinaigrette, whisk together the vinegar, mustard, 1 teaspoon salt, and ½ teaspoon pepper in a small bowl or measuring cup. Slowly whisk in the olive oil and pour over the salad. Add the Roquefort and walnuts and toss well. Sprinkle with salt and serve at room temperature.

EASY / PREP AHEAD

Sometimes the simplest thing is also the most elegant. This heirloom tomato salad of sliced tomatoes steeped in a little good red wine vinegar plus shards of blue cheese is one of the best examples of that. All I need to do is pick up a rotisserie chicken and dinner's served.

heirloom tomato & blue cheese salad

2 pounds heirloom tomatoes, cores removed

1 pint heirloom cherry tomatoes

Kosher salt and freshly ground black pepper

Good red wine vinegar

8 ounces good Roquefort, such as Société

Fresh basil leaves, torn or julienned

Good olive oil

SERVES 4

Slice the large tomatoes and arrange them on a platter. Cut the cherry tomatoes in half through the stem and arrange with the tomatoes. Sprinkle generously with salt and drizzle with vinegar. Set aside for 5 minutes.

Cut the cheese in slices and break into rough pieces, distributing the cheese over the tomatoes. Sprinkle with the basil leaves and drizzle with olive oil. Sprinkle with salt and pepper and serve at room temperature.

ASSEMBLED

I love to roast butternut squash until the edges caramelize. It's particularly delicious paired warm with creamy cold burrata. I serve it with big slices of toasted country bread and it makes a really good dinner.

caramelized butternut squash with burrata

3 pounds butternut squash, ¾-inch diced

Good olive oil

¼ cup light brown sugar, lightly packed

2 tablespoons (¼ stick) unsalted butter, diced

½ teaspoon crushed red pepper flakes

Kosher salt and freshly ground black pepper

¾ cup dried cranberries (3 ounces)

¾ cup dry Marsala wine

16 to 24 ounces burrata

⅓ cup roasted, salted Marcona almonds, coarsely chopped, for serving

2 ounces microgreens, for serving

Aged balsamic vinegar, for serving

SERVES 4

Preheat the oven to 400 degrees.

Place the butternut squash on a sheet pan with ¼ cup of olive oil, the brown sugar, butter, red pepper flakes, 1 tablespoon salt, and 1½ teaspoons black pepper. Toss well and spread out in one layer. Roast for 30 to 35 minutes, tossing every 10 minutes, until tender and the edges of the squash start to caramelize.

Meanwhile, place the cranberries and Marsala in a small saucepan, bring to a simmer over medium heat and cook for 2 minutes. Cover and set aside.

Place a quarter of the burrata in the center of each of four dinner plates. Toss the cranberries and almonds with the butternut squash and spoon the mixture around the cheese. Sprinkle with some microgreens, drizzle with balsamic vinegar and extra olive oil, and sprinkle with salt and black pepper. Serve while the squash is still warm.

PREP AHEAD

This dish turns simple scrambled eggs into the most elegant supper, first by cooking the eggs very, very slowly so they're creamy and light, and second, by stirring in cooked lobster and crabmeat at the end. This is easy to make yet still special enough to serve to your mother-in-law.

creamy eggs with lobster & crab

4 tablespoons (½ stick) unsalted butter, divided

½ red Holland bell pepper, small-diced

4 ounces cooked lobster meat, ½-inch diced

4 ounces cooked jumbo lump crabmeat

Kosher salt and freshly ground black pepper

2 tablespoons minced fresh chives, plus extra for serving

9 extra-large eggs

4 tablespoons heavy cream or half-and-half, divided

SERVES 3

Heat 2 tablespoons of the butter in a medium (10-inch) sauté pan over medium heat. Add the bell pepper and cook for 2 minutes. Add the lobster, crabmeat, ½ teaspoon salt, and ¼ teaspoon black pepper and cook for 2 to 3 minutes, until heated through. Stir in the chives and transfer to a bowl.

Meanwhile, heat the remaining 2 tablespoons butter in the pan over medium-low heat. In a large bowl, whisk together the eggs, 3 tablespoons of the cream, 1½ teaspoons salt, and ½ teaspoon black pepper. As soon as the butter melts, pour the egg mixture into the pan and cook slowly for 6 to 8 minutes, stirring rapidly with a rubber spatula, until the eggs start to become thick and creamy. Quickly fold the lobster-and-crab mixture into the eggs. Stir the remaining tablespoon of cream into the egg-and-seafood mixture, sprinkle with chives, salt and black pepper, and serve hot.

EASY

Panzanella is a great light dinner because, while of course you can follow the recipe exactly, you can also add anything you might have left over, such as roast chicken (page 128), cooked salmon (page 150), or even grilled steak (page 142). But no matter how you make it, the best part is always those toasted bread cubes drenched in mustard vinaigrette!

roasted shrimp panzanella

4 cups (1-inch) diced bread from a country loaf, crusts removed

1 cup good olive oil, divided

Kosher salt and freshly ground black pepper

1 pound (16 to 20-count) shrimp, peeled and deveined

¼ cup plus 2 tablespoons red wine vinegar

1 tablespoon minced garlic (3 cloves)

1 tablespoon Dijon mustard

1 hothouse cucumber, unpeeled, seeds removed, and ¾-inch diced

1 yellow Holland bell pepper, cored, seeded, and ¾-inch diced

1 red Holland bell pepper, cored, seeded, and ¾-inch diced

1 pint red cherry or grape tomatoes, halved through the stem

½ medium red onion, thinly sliced in half-rounds

¼ cup capers in brine, drained

3 ounces baby arugula

½ pound feta or ricotta salata, ¾-inch diced

SERVES 6

Preheat the oven to 400 degrees.

For the croutons, place the bread on a sheet pan, drizzle with 2 tablespoons olive oil, sprinkle with ½ teaspoon salt and ¼ teaspoon black pepper, toss together, and spread out in one layer. Bake for 10 minutes, tossing once, until lightly browned. Transfer to a bowl and set aside. Dry the shrimp. On the same sheet pan (no need to wash it), toss the shrimp with 2 tablespoons olive oil, 1 teaspoon salt, and ½ teaspoon black pepper. Spread out and roast for 7 minutes, until just pink and firm. Set aside.

Meanwhile, in a 1-cup glass measuring cup, whisk together the ¼ cup vinegar, the garlic, mustard, 1 teaspoon salt, and ½ teaspoon black pepper. While whisking, slowly add the remaining ¾ cup olive oil and set aside.

In a large bowl, combine the cucumber, bell peppers, tomatoes, red onion, capers, croutons, and shrimp. Pour enough vinaigrette over the mixture to moisten. Add the arugula, feta, and the remaining vinaigrette, and toss lightly. Sprinkle with the remaining 2 tablespoons vinegar and extra salt and serve at room temperature.

PREP AHEAD

In the winter, when salad ingredients are less than exciting, this orange and fennel salad never fails to wow. The sweet, colorful varieties of oranges are so delicious with the anise flavor of the thinly sliced fennel plus a sprinkling of fresh mint and basil. Yum! With some cooked shrimp from the seafood shop, you've got dinner.

provençal orange salad

½ small red onion

3 seedless oranges, such as Cara Cara or navel

3 blood oranges

½ fennel bulb, top and core removed

10 large green olives, such as picholine or Castelvetrano, pitted

1½ tablespoons julienned fresh mint leaves

1½ tablespoons julienned fresh basil leaves

Good olive oil

Kosher salt and freshly ground black pepper

Fleur de sel or sea salt, for serving

SERVES 4

Slice the onion crosswise in very thin half-rounds, place in a small bowl, and cover with ice water for 15 minutes. (This softens the pungency of the raw onion and makes a big difference in the salad.) Drain and set aside.

Meanwhile, cut the ends off all the oranges with a serrated knife and stand each one on a flat end. Slice down the side of each orange to remove all the peel and white pith, then slice each orange crosswise in ⅓-inch-thick rounds, discarding any seeds. Place the oranges and all the juices on a platter.

Slice the fennel crosswise very thinly by hand or with a mandoline, and distribute the fennel slices on the oranges. Sprinkle on the drained red onion, the olives, mint, basil, 3 tablespoons olive oil, 1 teaspoon kosher salt, and ½ teaspoon pepper. Toss gently, taste for seasonings, sprinkle with fleur de sel, and serve at room temperature.

I order the best oranges from thesistersmarket.com.

ASSEMBLED

We know Julia Child made everything better—even potato salad! For this dish, she used the trick Italians use for pasta—she added some of the potato cooking water to the salad to make a creamier sauce and then added celery, shallots, cornichons, and dill. As she would say, "Delicious!"

potato salad à la julia child

2 pounds large Yukon Gold potatoes, peeled and sliced ½-inch thick

Kosher salt and freshly ground black pepper

2 tablespoons good Champagne or white wine vinegar

¾ cup medium-diced celery (2 to 3 ribs)

½ cup medium-diced shallots (2 large)

¼ cup drained, chopped cornichons

¼ cup chopped fresh chives

¼ cup chopped fresh dill, plus extra for serving

⅔ cup good mayonnaise, such as Hellmann's or Best

⅓ cup sour cream

2 hard-boiled eggs, cooled and large-diced (see note)

SERVES 6

Place the potatoes in a large saucepan with water to cover by 2 inches. Add 2 tablespoons salt and bring to a boil. Lower the heat and simmer for 10 to 12 minutes, until just barely tender when pierced with a fork. Set aside ⅓ cup of the cooking liquid, then drain the potatoes and place them in a large bowl. Drizzle the potatoes with the vinegar and reserved cooking liquid and let them stand for 10 minutes, tossing occasionally.

Meanwhile, in a medium bowl, combine the celery, shallots, cornichons, chives, and dill and set aside. In a small bowl, whisk together the mayonnaise, sour cream, 1 teaspoon salt, and ½ teaspoon pepper. Add three quarters of the vegetable-and-herb mixture to the potatoes, reserving the rest. Stir in the mayonnaise dressing, incorporating any liquid in the bowl, and cool to room temperature. Cover and refrigerate for at least 2 hours for the flavors to blend.

When ready to serve, add the reserved vegetable mixture and the eggs to the salad and sprinkle with extra dill, salt, and pepper. Stir gently to combine. Taste for seasonings and serve cold or at room temperature.

For perfectly cooked hard-boiled eggs, bring a pot of water to a boil and carefully lower the eggs into the water. Reduce the heat and simmer (the shells will crack if they bang against each other) for exactly 10 minutes. Remove the eggs, run under cool water, and peel.

MAKE AHEAD

This is hardly a recipe, but that's exactly the point! The key to this non-recipe is to make sure you use the ripest melon and the best Italian prosciutto di Parma and you'll have a light dinner that is really special. This dish is usually served with the prosciutto wrapped around each piece of melon but it's so pretty served more casually, so why bother??

melon & prosciutto

1 large ripe cantaloupe

6 ounces thinly sliced Italian prosciutto di Parma

Coarse sea salt and freshly ground black pepper

2 lemons, cut in quarters

SERVES 4

Cut off the ends of the cantaloupe and stand it upright on a cutting board. With a sharp knife, cut off the rind starting at the top and slicing down to the bottom, going all the way around the melon. Slice in half vertically and discard the seeds. Place the cut sides of each half down on the board and cut crosswise ½ inch thick. On each of four dinner plates, artfully arrange a quarter of the cantaloupe. Ripple slices of prosciutto down the middle of the cantaloupe and sprinkle with salt and pepper. Squeeze some lemon juice on each serving and serve at room temperature.

ASSEMBLED

ploughman's lunch

A traditional English ploughman's lunch originated from the meal that a farmer would bring to the fields to eat at midday, usually a piece of cheese, a hunk of bread, and maybe some pickled onions. At some point, English pubs started serving full ploughman's lunch boards around the theme but added specialties like ham, sausage, or pork pie, plus condiments like pickled onions, celery, and chutney. It was a great meal to offer because nothing needed to be cooked to order, which is why it's also an easy meal to serve for a light dinner. I'm not sure how traditionally English mine is but I love to include hard-boiled or jammy eggs, aged sharp English Cheddar, some Stilton, crusty bread, honey-baked ham, a big slice of coarse pâté, sweet fig preserves, spicy chutney, plus a green salad or some vegetables like radishes and celery.

This is a list of things you can buy that will make a great "ploughman's lunch" for dinner:

Grilled slices of country bread	Cherry tomatoes
Aged English Cheddar	Mini cucumbers
English Stilton	Chutney
Honey-glazed ham, sliced	Mustard
Country pâté	Fig preserves
Sausages	Dried apricots
Meat pies	Fresh figs
Jammy eggs	Clementines
Celery stalks	

ASSEMBLED

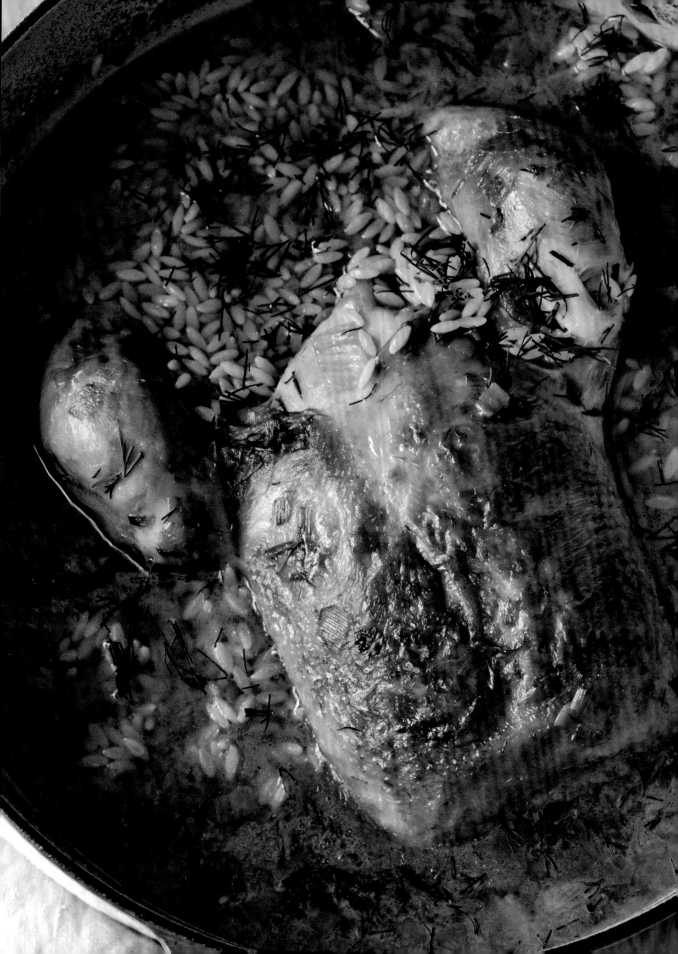

family dinners

CONTENTS CONTINUES >>

Salmon Teriyaki & Broccolini

Mussels with Saffron Cream

Overnight Mac & Cheese

One-Pot Oven Risotto

Mushroom Bolognese

Weeknight Spaghettoni with
Tomatoes & Pancetta

Lemon Linguine with Zucchini
& Basil

Orange Marmalade–Glazed Ham

prep ahead!

I'm a morning person. It always amazes me how restaurant cooks and chefs can start work at 3 p.m. and go until the wee hours of the next morning—I would simply die of exhaustion. But I think food that's prepared just before serving tastes better than reheated food, so for years, I would spend the entire day waiting to cook for a party like a dog on a racetrack at the starting gate. By the time I actually *started* cooking, I was completely exhausted and all I wanted to do was go lie down and take a nap.

Now I avoid that problem by choosing recipes that I can prep either partially or entirely ahead of time and then throw the whole thing in the oven before dinner. Not only have I done all the serious work ahead, but all the cooking dishes have been washed and put away so I'm totally ready to have a good time with my friends.

The trick is knowing which elements of a recipe you can make ahead and when to combine them for the best texture, flavor, and color. For example, for the Salmon Teriyaki & Broccolini (page 150), the salmon, the broccolini, and the teriyaki sauce can all be prepped ahead of time, but if you combine the sauce and the salmon in advance, the soy sauce will break down the fish and change its texture. If you simply pour the sauce over the salmon right before you throw it in the oven with the broccolini though, no problem!

Other recipes, like Chicken in a Pot with Orzo (page 131), can be made a full day before serving (stews and soups reheat really well), but if you add the orzo before you store it, it will become too soft and absorb all of the delicious broth. Instead I prepare the stew just to the point of adding the orzo, then reheat the stew before dinner, add the orzo, turn off the heat, and allow it to sit for 20 to 25 minutes, until the orzo is tender. No hassle and dinner is served!

Prepping vegetables is a great way to get ahead but you need to store them properly to keep them really fresh. (The exception is potatoes, which need to be cut at the last minute or they'll turn brown.) For the Hasselback Kielbasa (page 139), after I prep the kielbasa and combine the sauce ingredients, I'll cut the onions, fennel, and bell peppers and refrigerate them in a sealable plastic bag with a slightly damp paper towel to keep them moist. At dinnertime, all I need to do is roast the vegetables, add the kielbasa, and brush it with the honey mustard. A delicious dinner and not at all exhausting.

Throughout the book, I've noted which recipes can be prepped ahead, made ahead, and even assembled ahead so you can be relaxed and happy when the doorbell rings.

A simple roast chicken is famously my go-to dinner but I like to have variations up my sleeve to make it more seasonal. This version with carrots, potatoes, and asparagus is a whole meal in a roasting pan. The pan juices drizzled over the chicken and vegetables make it even better.

roast chicken with spring vegetables

1 (4-pound) whole chicken

Kosher salt and freshly ground black pepper

1 lemon, quartered

6 sprigs fresh thyme, divided

6 sprigs fresh rosemary, divided

3 tablespoons unsalted butter, melted

½ pound heirloom baby carrots, scrubbed (12 to 14)

1 pound Yukon Gold potatoes, scrubbed, 1-inch diced

1 large yellow onion, cut into 8 wedges through the stem

8 garlic cloves, unpeeled

Good olive oil

12 to 14 asparagus, woody ends removed, cut diagonally in 2-inch pieces

SERVES 3 TO 4

Preheat the oven to 425 degrees.

Pat the chicken dry with paper towels and place it in a large (13 × 16-inch) roasting pan. Sprinkle the cavity generously with salt and place the lemon, 2 sprigs of thyme, and 2 sprigs of rosemary in the cavity. Tie the legs together with kitchen string and tuck the wings under the body. Brush the outside with the butter and sprinkle generously with salt and pepper.

In a large bowl, combine the carrots, potatoes, onion, garlic, ⅓ cup olive oil, 1 teaspoon salt, and ½ teaspoon pepper. Transfer the vegetables to the pan with the chicken and place the remaining sprigs of thyme and rosemary on the vegetables.

Roast for 20 minutes, then reduce the heat to 350 degrees and roast for 40 to 50 minutes, tossing the vegetables in the pan juices from time to time. Roast until an instant-read thermometer registers 165 degrees in the breast and 175 degrees in the thigh. Leaving the oven on, transfer the chicken to a carving board, cover it loosely with aluminum foil, and allow to rest for 12 to 15 minutes.

Meanwhile, add the asparagus to the pan, tossing them with the other vegetables. Roast for 10 to 12 minutes, until the asparagus are crisp-tender. Discard the herb branches, carve the chicken, and serve with the vegetables and pan juices.

TWO-FER: *Shred or dice any leftover chicken and add to the Warm Vegetable & Grain Bowl (page 98) and add the bones to the pot when making Homemade Chicken Stock (page 83).*

EASY

I've been tinkering with a recipe for old-fashioned chicken in a pot for years but they all come out just tasting like chicken soup. Nigella Lawson's wonderful cookbook Cook, Eat, Repeat *inspired me to brown the chicken first, which adds lots of flavor, and then add orzo to thicken the broth.*

chicken in a pot with orzo

Good olive oil

1 (3½ to 4-pound) whole chicken

2 cups (¾-inch diced) scrubbed carrots (10 ounces)

2 cups (¾-inch) diced celery (4 ribs)

2 cups chopped leeks, white and light green parts (3 leeks) (see note)

2 cups chopped fennel, stalks and core removed (1 large bulb)

2 teaspoons minced garlic (2 cloves)

4 cups simmering chicken stock, preferably homemade (page 83)

½ teaspoon saffron threads

6 sprigs fresh thyme

8 sprigs fresh parsley

10 sprigs fresh dill, plus extra for serving

Kosher salt and freshly ground black pepper

¾ cup orzo

SERVES 4

Soak the diced leeks in water to remove any dirt and spin-dry.

Prepare completely, except the orzo. Reheat to simmering, add the orzo, and continue with the recipe.

MAKE AHEAD

Preheat the oven to 350 degrees.

Heat 3 tablespoons of olive oil in a medium (11-inch) Dutch oven, such as Le Creuset, over medium to medium-high heat. Dry the chicken all over, place it in the pot breast side down, and sear it for 5 to 7 minutes without moving, until the skin is nicely browned. Turn the chicken breast side up and sear for another 4 to 5 minutes, until browned on the bottom. Transfer the chicken to a plate.

Add the carrots, celery, leeks, and fennel to the pot and sauté for 10 to 15 minutes, stirring occasionally, until the vegetables start to brown. Add the garlic and cook for one minute. Return the chicken to the pot, breast side up, spreading the vegetables around the chicken. Add the chicken stock, saffron, and enough water to cover the chicken with just an inch of the breastbone exposed. Tie the thyme, parsley, and dill together in a bundle with kitchen string and add to the pot along with 1½ tablespoons salt and 1½ teaspoons pepper. Bring to a boil, cover, and bake for 1 hour and 15 minutes, checking to be sure the liquid is simmering.

Discard the herb bundle, stir the orzo into the broth, cover, and allow to sit off the heat for 20 to 25 minutes, until the orzo is tender. Using forks to separate the chicken into quarters, carefully pull the breast meat away from the bones (I leave the bones in the leg portion) and reheat, if necessary. Spoon some of the chicken, broth, and pasta into large shallow bowls, and serve hot sprinkled generously with minced dill and salt.

This is a really easy dinner to prepare but special enough to serve to company. The chicken thighs are roasted and then nestled in a sauce of onions, leeks, and crème fraîche.

creamy chicken thighs with lemon & thyme

3 pounds bone-in, skin-on chicken thighs (6 to 8 thighs)

Good olive oil

Kosher salt and freshly ground black pepper

2 tablespoons (¼ stick) unsalted butter

1½ cups chopped yellow onion (1 large)

1½ cups chopped leeks, white and light green parts (2 leeks) (see note, page 131)

2 teaspoons minced garlic (2 cloves)

½ cup good chicken stock, preferably homemade (page 83)

½ cup dry white wine, such as Pinot Grigio

½ cup crème fraîche

2 tablespoons freshly squeezed lemon juice

½ small lemon, sliced in thin half-rounds

8 to 10 sprigs fresh thyme

Cooked basmati rice (page 153) or couscous, for serving

SERVES 4

Preheat the oven to 400 degrees.

Place the chicken on a sheet pan, skin side up, and dry with paper towels. Rub with olive oil and sprinkle generously with salt and pepper. Roast for 30 to 40 minutes, until cooked through and the skin is golden brown. Set aside.

Meanwhile, heat the butter and 2 tablespoons of olive oil in a large (12-inch) ovenproof sauté pan over medium heat. Add the onion and leeks and sauté for 5 to 7 minutes, until tender. Add the garlic and cook for 2 minutes. Add the chicken stock and wine and simmer for 5 minutes. Whisk in the crème fraîche, lemon juice, 2 teaspoons salt, and ½ teaspoon pepper and taste for seasonings.

Nestle the chicken thighs into the sauce in the sauté pan. Tuck the lemon slices among the thighs and strew the thyme sprigs on top. Place the pan in the oven and roast uncovered for 15 minutes. Serve hot with the sauce over rice or couscous.

MAKE AHEAD

Pork tenderloins are not hard to prepare but this method is crazy easy. You season the tenderloins with lots of rosemary and salt and put them in a very hot oven for exactly 5½ minutes, then turn off the oven and let them sit for an hour. Perfectly cooked tenderloins every time!

rosemary roasted pork tenderloins

2 pork tenderloins, trimmed (1¼ pounds each)

Good olive oil

2 tablespoons coarsely chopped fresh rosemary

Flaked sea salt, such as Maldon

Freshly ground black pepper

Mango chutney, for serving

SERVES 6

Preheat the oven to 500 degrees (make sure your oven is clean!). Place an oven rack in the top third of the oven. Allow the tenderloins to sit at room temperature for 30 minutes.

Place the tenderloins smooth side up 1½ inches apart on a sheet pan. Pat the meat dry with paper towels. Generously brush the tenderloins with 3 tablespoons olive oil, then sprinkle with the rosemary, 1 tablespoon sea salt, and 1 teaspoon pepper. Tuck the thin "tail" ends under and tie them with kitchen string so the tenderloins are an even thickness.

Place the tenderloins on the prepared oven rack and roast for **exactly** 5½ minutes. Turn off the oven and let the pork stay in the oven for one hour **without opening the door**. Transfer the tenderloins to a cutting board and slice thickly. Sprinkle with salt and serve warm with the mango chutney.

EASY

Meatballs are a really great component for a satisfying dinner; they can be served on their own, on a puddle of Parmesan Polenta (page 194), with cooked pasta, or in a hero sandwich. The two things that make these special are first, roasting them, and second, using really good Parmesan and Pecorino.

veal meatballs

½ cup good olive oil, divided

2 teaspoons minced garlic (2 cloves)

1 pound ground veal (see note)

1 pound ground pork (see note)

½ pound sweet Italian sausage, casings removed and meat crumbled

1 cup Italian-style breadcrumbs, such as Progresso

½ cup grated Italian Parmesan cheese (2 ounces)

¼ cup grated Italian Pecorino cheese (1 ounce)

½ cup minced fresh parsley

1 teaspoon ground fennel

Kosher salt and freshly ground black pepper

2 extra-large eggs, lightly beaten

¾ cup whole milk

¾ cup fresh whole-milk ricotta

2 (32-ounce) jars good marinara sauce, such as Rao's

MAKES 22 MEATBALLS / SERVES 6 TO 8

Preheat the oven to 425 degrees. Arrange two racks evenly spaced in the oven.

Heat ¼ cup of olive oil in a small (8-inch) sauté pan over medium-low heat. Add the garlic and sauté for 30 seconds, until fragrant but not browned. Set aside.

Place the veal, pork, and sausage in a large mixing bowl. Add the breadcrumbs, Parmesan, Pecorino, parsley, fennel, 1½ tablespoons salt, and 2 teaspoons pepper and blend lightly with a fork. Add the eggs, milk, ricotta, and the garlic-and-oil mixture and combine lightly but thoroughly.

Measure 2½ to 3-ounce portions of the mixture (I use a level 2¼-inch ice cream scoop) and with damp hands roll each portion lightly into a ball. Place the meatballs one inch apart on two sheet pans. Brush generously with the remaining ¼ cup olive oil. Roast the meatballs for 25 to 30 minutes, until lightly browned.

Pour the marinara sauce into a large pot and bring to a simmer. Gently add the meatballs and simmer for 10 minutes. Serve hot.

Finely ground meat makes moister meatballs. If the veal and pork are coarsely ground, put them in a food processor fitted with the steel blade and pulse a few times until finely ground.

Prep the meatballs a day ahead and roast them before serving or prepare them completely and freeze them in the sauce.

PREP AHEAD / MAKE AHEAD

Sam Sifton published a recipe for Hasselback Kielbasa in the New York Times *and my friend Peter Wallace served me his take on it for dinner. I took it a step further, adding lots of vegetables and herbs but the original idea is purely Sam's. When I'm in a hurry, this is go-to goodness.*

hasselback kielbasa

¾ pound yellow onions (2 to 3 onions)

1 (1-pound) fennel bulb, stalks removed

1 each red, yellow, and orange Holland bell pepper

Good olive oil

2 tablespoons minced garlic (6 cloves)

2 teaspoons minced fresh thyme leaves, plus extra sprigs

1 teaspoon whole fennel seeds, chopped

Kosher salt and freshly ground black pepper

2 pounds fully cooked, smoked kielbasa

¼ cup Dijon mustard

¼ cup liquid honey

SERVES 6

Preheat the oven to 425 degrees.

Cut the onions in half, slice them crosswise in ½-inch-thick half-rounds, and place them in a large bowl. Cut the fennel bulb in half lengthwise, cut the halves in 1-inch-thick wedges through the core (to keep the wedges intact) and add to the bowl. Cut the peppers in 1-inch-wide strips, discarding the stems and seeds, and add to the bowl. Toss with 4 tablespoons olive oil, the garlic, thyme, fennel seeds, 2 teaspoons salt, and 1 teaspoon black pepper. Transfer the vegetables to a very large (14 × 18-inch) roasting pan (or two sheet pans), spread them evenly in a single layer, and roast for 20 minutes, tossing once with a large metal spatula.

Meanwhile, cut the kielbasa crosswise in ¼-inch-thick slices, being careful to cut only two thirds of the way through. When the vegetables are ready, toss them again, discard the thyme branches, and place the kielbasa on top. Combine the mustard and honey and brush the top and sides of the kielbasa. Roast for 30 minutes, brushing the kielbasa with the honey mustard every 10 minutes, until it is crispy and browned. (Reserve extra honey mustard for serving.) Sprinkle the vegetables with salt and serve hot with the reserved honey mustard on the side.

TWO-FER: *Add leftover sausage to the Tuscan White Bean Soup (page 91) or any bean, lentil, or split pea soup.*

EASY / PREP AHEAD

The difference between a porterhouse and a T-bone steak is that the porterhouse has a larger "filet" portion than the T-bone so it's a little more expensive. This is a luxurious dinner for a party and so celebratory. I make the herbed oil in advance so all I need to do is grill the steak before dinner. This was inspired by my favorite steak at Lilia in Williamsburg, Brooklyn.

grilled porterhouse steak with rosemary & fennel

1 (2-inch-thick) dry-aged porterhouse steak (2 to 2¼ pounds) (see note)

Good olive oil

Kosher salt and freshly ground black pepper

2 teaspoons minced garlic (2 cloves)

1 tablespoon minced fresh rosemary

2 teaspoons ground fennel

SERVES 4

Allow the steak to sit at room temperature for one hour before you grill it.

Prepare a fire in a charcoal grill, mounding all the coals on one side of the grill to make a hot side and a cool side. Brush the steak all over with 2 tablespoons olive oil and sprinkle it on both sides with 2 teaspoons salt. Sear the steak over the hot coals for 2 minutes on one side without moving it at all, then turn the steak and sear the other side for 2 minutes. Transfer the steak to the cool side of the grill and close the lid, making sure the vents are open so the fire doesn't go out. Cook the steak for 10 to 12 minutes, until the internal temperature is 115 to 120 degrees for rare and 125 degrees for medium-rare. Transfer to a plate to rest.

Meanwhile, prepare the herb oil. Place ¼ cup of olive oil and the garlic in a small saucepan. Place it over medium-low heat and watch closely until the garlic starts to sizzle. Continue cooking **for 15 to 30 seconds,** until the garlic becomes fragrant but not browned. Turn off the heat, add the rosemary, fennel, 1 teaspoon salt, and ½ teaspoon pepper and set aside.

As soon as the steak comes off the grill, brush half of the herb oil on top, turn, and brush the rest on the other side. Cover the plate with aluminum foil and allow to rest for 10 minutes. Slice the steak and serve warm.

Pat LaFrieda's dry-aged porterhouse steaks, which you can order online, are amazing.

PREP AHEAD

This is summer in a skillet—a one-pot dinner with clams, sausage, corn, and tomatoes. The whole meal is ready in 15 minutes and I just bring the skillet to the table so everyone can help themselves. Don't forget to serve good bread for dunking in the butter and wine sauce!

summer skillet with clams, sausage & corn

Good olive oil

1½ cups small-diced yellow onion (1 large)

¾ pound sweet Italian sausage, casings removed

3 cups fresh corn kernels, cut off the cob (4 to 5 ears)

1 pound vine-ripened tomatoes, ½-inch diced

½ teaspoon crushed red pepper flakes

Kosher salt and freshly ground black pepper

½ cup dry white wine, such as Pinot Grigio

2 tablespoons (¼ stick) unsalted butter, large-diced

32 fresh littleneck clams, scrubbed (see note)

3 tablespoons julienned fresh basil leaves

French bread, for serving

SERVES 4

In a large (12-inch) cast iron skillet, heat 2 tablespoons of olive oil over medium heat. Add the onion and sauté over medium-low for 4 to 5 minutes, stirring occasionally, until tender. Add the sausage, breaking it into bite-size pieces, and cook for 6 to 8 minutes, stirring occasionally, until the sausage is no longer pink.

Add the corn, tomatoes, red pepper flakes, 2 teaspoons salt, and 1 teaspoon black pepper to the skillet and sauté for 3 minutes. Pour in the wine and scatter the butter on top. Nestle the clams into the vegetable-and-sausage mixture, hinged sides down, in tight concentric circles. Bring to a boil, cover the skillet, lower the heat, and simmer for 8 to 12 minutes, just until the clams open.

Ladle into shallow bowls, sprinkle with the basil, and serve hot with the French bread.

To clean clams, soak them in a bowl of cool water for 15 minutes.

EASY

A southern shrimp boil is something like a New England clambake but less complicated to prepare. While it's usually boiled in a large pot of water, I roasted everything together and came up with a really good, easy dinner. It's a little spicy, which calls for serving it with ice-cold beer!

oven-roasted southern "shrimp boil"

1 pound small (1-inch diameter) Yukon Gold potatoes, halved

Good olive oil

Old Bay Seasoning

Kosher salt and freshly ground black pepper

3 ears corn, husked and cut crosswise in 1½-inch chunks (see note)

1 pound smoked kielbasa, sliced ½-inch-thick diagonally

1½ pounds large (16 to 20-count) shrimp in the shell

2½ tablespoons minced fresh parsley

2 lemons

SERVES 4

If the corn is starchy, boil it for 3 to 5 minutes before adding it to the pan.

EASY

Preheat the oven to 425 degrees.

In a large (13 × 16-inch) roasting pan, toss the potatoes with 1½ tablespoons olive oil, 1½ teaspoons Old Bay Seasoning, ½ teaspoon salt, and ¼ teaspoon pepper. Spread the potatoes in a single layer, cut sides down, and roast for 12 minutes.

Meanwhile, place the corn in a medium bowl, add 1½ tablespoons olive oil, 1½ teaspoons Old Bay Seasoning, ½ teaspoon salt, and ¼ teaspoon pepper and toss well. When the potatoes have cooked for 12 minutes, turn them with a small spatula and spread out in the pan. Add the corn and kielbasa and roast for 10 minutes.

Meanwhile, place the shrimp in the same bowl and toss with 1½ tablespoons olive oil, 2 teaspoons Old Bay seasoning, ½ teaspoon salt, and ¼ teaspoon pepper. Add the shrimp to the pan and roast for 10 to 15 minutes longer, tossing halfway through with a large metal spatula, until the shrimp are just cooked.

Sprinkle with the parsley and the juice of one lemon. Cut the second lemon in wedges. Serve hot in large bowls with the lemon wedges and an extra bowl for discarding the corn cobs and shells.

This is my go-to weeknight dinner. The salmon is drizzled with a soy, maple, and ginger glaze and roasted for about 12 minutes. The broccolini roasts right alongside for 10 minutes, while the basmati rice steams on top of the stove at the same time. How easy (and delish) is that??

salmon teriyaki & broccolini

Good olive oil

3 tablespoons soy sauce, such as Kikkoman (see note)

1½ tablespoons pure maple syrup

2 teaspoons toasted sesame oil

1 tablespoon minced fresh ginger

1 tablespoon minced garlic (3 cloves)

¼ teaspoon crushed red pepper flakes

4 skinless salmon fillets (2 to 2½ pounds total)

Kosher salt and freshly ground black pepper

1½ pounds broccolini, lower thirds of the stems discarded

Steamed Basmati Rice (recipe follows)

SERVES 4

Preheat the oven to 400 degrees. Arrange two racks evenly spaced in the oven.

In a small saucepan, combine 3 tablespoons of olive oil, the soy sauce, maple syrup, sesame oil, ginger, garlic, and red pepper flakes. Bring to a boil over medium heat, lower the heat, and simmer for just 2 minutes. Set aside.

Arrange the salmon, rounded sides up, in a baking dish just large enough to hold them with a little space between the fillets. Sprinkle with 1 teaspoon salt and ½ teaspoon black pepper and spoon the soy sauce mixture evenly over the fillets. Roast on the upper rack for 12 to 13 minutes for rare or 13 to 14 minutes for medium, depending on the thickness of the fillets.

At the same time, place the broccolini on a sheet pan, drizzle it with 4 tablespoons olive oil and sprinkle with 1½ teaspoons salt and ¾ teaspoon black pepper. Toss with your hands and spread out in one layer. Roast the broccolini on the lower oven rack for 10 to 12 minutes, tossing once, until crisp-tender.

Place the salmon, broccolini, and basmati rice on four plates and spoon the pan juices over the salmon. Serve hot.

I use regular—not low-sodium—soy sauce.

EASY

Following the cooking directions on the rice package tends to result in rice that is overcooked for my taste. I prefer when it is al dente, like pasta, with a little resistance "to the tooth."

steamed basmati rice

1½ cups white long-grain basmati rice, such as Rice Select

1 tablespoon unsalted butter

Kosher salt

SERVES 4 TO 6

Combine 2½ cups water, the rice, butter, and 2 teaspoons salt in a medium saucepan. Bring the water to a boil over medium heat, lower the heat, cover, and simmer for **just** 10 minutes. (You may have to pull the pot halfway off the burner to keep the rice at a simmer.) Turn off the heat and allow the rice to sit, covered, for 3 to 5 minutes, until just cooked through. Fluff with a fork and serve hot.

EASY

There's nothing like a big bowl of steamed mussels for dinner served along with their delicious wine and saffron cooking broth for dipping French bread. Any leftover mussels are wonderful added to One-Pot Oven Risotto (page 158) and they also make nice appetizers served with a little herbed mayonnaise.

mussels with saffron cream

2 tablespoons (¼ stick) unsalted butter

½ cup chopped shallots (2 shallots)

1 tablespoon minced garlic (3 cloves)

1 teaspoon saffron threads

1½ cups dry white wine, such as Pinot Grigio, divided

1 cup heavy cream

1 teaspoon grated lemon zest

2 teaspoons minced fresh tarragon leaves

Kosher salt and freshly ground black pepper

4 pounds fresh mussels, scrubbed and debearded (see note)

2 tablespoons minced fresh parsley

2 tablespoons minced fresh chives

Crusty baguette, for serving

SERVES 4

Melt the butter in a large (12-inch-round) pot or Dutch oven, such as Le Creuset, over medium-low heat. Add the shallots, garlic, and saffron and sauté for 4 minutes, until the shallots are tender and the garlic is fragrant. Add ½ cup of the wine, the cream, lemon zest, and tarragon. Bring to a boil, lower the heat, and simmer for 8 to 10 minutes, until slightly thickened. Stir in 2 teaspoons salt and 1 teaspoon pepper.

Add the remaining 1 cup of wine plus ½ cup of water. Add the mussels, cover the pot, and bring to a boil over medium heat. Lower the heat and simmer for 4 to 5 minutes, until all the mussels have opened (discard any that don't open). Sprinkle with the parsley, chives, and 1 teaspoon salt. Stir well with a large metal spoon and serve hot in shallow bowls with the broth and bread for dipping.

Many seafood shops sell cleaned mussels; if yours aren't, pull off and discard the stringy beards. To be safe, I soak the mussels in a large bowl of water with some flour so they disgorge any sand. Discard any mussels that don't close when you tap them.

EASY

This is the easiest, cheesiest, crustiest mac & cheese I've ever made! It's the perfect prep-ahead dish; you don't even need to make a roux. Prepare the mixture a day ahead, refrigerate it overnight, pour it into an ovenproof dish, and bake it before dinner.

overnight mac & cheese

Kosher salt and freshly ground black pepper

12 ounces cavatappi pasta

4½ cups heavy cream

3 cups grated Gruyère cheese, divided (8 ounces)

1½ cups grated sharp white Cheddar, such as Cabot, divided (4 ounces)

½ teaspoon ground nutmeg

3 tablespoons melted unsalted butter, plus extra for the dish

2½ cups fresh white breadcrumbs (see note)

SERVES 6

A day before you plan to serve, bring a large pot of water to a boil. Add 2 tablespoons salt and the pasta and cook for 4 minutes (it will be undercooked). Drain (don't rinse) and set aside.

Meanwhile, in a medium (10-inch) bowl, combine the cream, 1½ cups of the Gruyère, ¾ cup of the Cheddar, the nutmeg, 1 tablespoon salt, and 1½ teaspoons pepper. Stir the hot pasta into the cream mixture, cover the bowl with plastic, and refrigerate for 24 hours. The pasta will absorb the cream and expand.

When ready to bake, allow the mixture to sit at room temperature for about one hour. (You can also microwave it for 4 minutes.) Preheat the oven to 400 degrees.

Butter a 9 × 13 × 2-inch baking dish. Stir the pasta mixture well, transfer it to the dish, and spread it evenly. Combine the remaining 1½ cups Gruyère and ¾ cup Cheddar and sprinkle evenly on top. Combine the breadcrumbs and the 3 tablespoons melted butter and sprinkle evenly over the cheese. Bake for 20 to 25 minutes, rotating halfway through, until golden brown. Serve hot.

For 2½ cups of breadcrumbs, remove the crusts from 6 slices of white bread and dice. Place in the bowl of a food processor fitted with the steel blade and process until finely ground.

PREP AHEAD

You could stand at the stove stirring risotto for 25 to 30 minutes, or you could combine the ingredients in a Dutch oven, throw it in the oven for 35 minutes, and spend the time doing something much more fun. I know which I would choose! Asparagus, saffron, wine, and Parmesan make this risotto particularly satisfying.

one-pot oven risotto

Good olive oil

1¼ cups thinly sliced shallots (2 large)

1 pound fresh asparagus, tough ends removed, cut diagonally in 1-inch lengths (see note)

1½ cups Arborio rice (10 ounces)

5 to 6 cups simmering chicken stock, preferably homemade (page 83)

½ teaspoon saffron threads

½ cup dry white wine

1 cup freshly grated Italian Parmesan cheese, plus extra for serving

3 tablespoons unsalted butter, diced

Kosher salt and freshly ground black pepper

SERVES 4

Preheat the oven to 350 degrees.

In a medium (11-inch) Dutch oven, such as Le Creuset, heat 2 tablespoons olive oil over medium heat. Add the shallots and cook for 2 minutes. Add the asparagus and cook for 5 minutes, stirring occasionally, until al dente. Transfer to a bowl and set aside.

In the same Dutch oven, heat one additional tablespoon olive oil. Add the rice and stir to coat the rice with oil. Add 4 cups of the chicken stock and the saffron, bring to a simmer, and cover. Transfer to the oven and bake for 35 minutes, until the rice is tender and the liquid is absorbed.

Remove from the oven and add the white wine, stirring well until incorporated, then add one more cup of chicken stock, the Parmesan, butter, 2½ teaspoons salt, and 1 teaspoon pepper. Stir vigorously with a wooden spoon for 2 to 3 minutes, until the risotto is thick and creamy, adding more chicken stock, if necessary, to keep the risotto very creamy. Stir in the asparagus-and-shallot mixture and serve hot sprinkled with extra grated Parmesan.

To reheat, add a little white wine and reheat in individual bowls in the microwave. Sprinkle with Parmesan and serve hot.

Instead of asparagus, you can use broccolini, broccoli, snow peas, or snap peas; or you can add frozen peas just before serving.

EASY

My assistant Kristina Felix wanted to make a vegetarian pasta for dinner so she substituted cremini mushrooms for the ground sirloin in my Weeknight Bolognese and came up with a delicious meatless dinner!

mushroom bolognese

Good olive oil

1½ pounds cremini mushrooms, brushed clean, trimmed, medium-diced

4 teaspoons minced garlic (4 cloves)

1 tablespoon minced fresh oregano leaves

¼ teaspoon crushed red pepper flakes

1¼ cups dry red wine, such as Chianti, divided

1 (28-ounce) can crushed tomatoes, preferably San Marzano

2 tablespoons tomato paste

Kosher salt and freshly ground black pepper

1 pound dried pasta, such as large shells or rigatoni

¼ teaspoon ground nutmeg

¼ cup chopped fresh basil leaves, lightly packed, plus more for serving

¼ cup Italian mascarpone cheese

½ cup freshly grated Italian Parmesan cheese, plus extra for serving

SERVES 4 TO 6

Heat 2 tablespoons of olive oil in a medium (10-inch) Dutch oven, such as Le Creuset, over medium heat. Add the mushrooms and cook for 5 to 7 minutes, until starting to brown. Stir in the garlic, oregano, and red pepper flakes and cook for one minute. Pour 1 cup of the wine into the pot and stir to scrape up any browned bits. Stir in the tomatoes, tomato paste, 1 tablespoon salt, and 1½ teaspoons black pepper. Bring to a boil, then lower the heat and simmer for 10 minutes.

Meanwhile, bring a large pot of water to a boil. Add 2 tablespoons salt and the pasta and cook al dente according to the directions on the box. Drain, reserving 1 cup of the cooking water.

Add the remaining ¼ cup of wine, the nutmeg, basil, and mascarpone to the sauce and simmer for 5 minutes. Add the pasta and enough of the reserved pasta water to make a loose sauce and cook over low heat for 3 minutes, until the pasta has absorbed the sauce. Add a bit more cooking water if it's too thick. Off the heat, stir in the ½ cup of Parmesan. Serve hot sprinkled with extra Parmesan and basil.

MAKE AHEAD

Everyone needs a few quick pasta dinners in their repertoire, and this one is really adaptable. It's wonderful as is, but you could also serve it with Veal Meatballs (page 136) one night and with a big dollop of ricotta the next. The pancetta and red wine give it fantastic flavor.

weeknight spaghettoni with tomatoes & pancetta

Kosher salt and freshly ground black pepper

Good olive oil

6 ounces (¼-inch) diced pancetta

1½ cups chopped yellow onion (1 large)

2 teaspoons minced garlic (2 cloves)

½ teaspoon crushed red pepper flakes

½ cup dry red wine, such as Chianti

1 (14.5-ounce) can crushed San Marzano tomatoes

1½ teaspoons sugar

1 pound dried spaghettoni or bucatini (see note)

1 cup freshly grated Italian Pecorino cheese, divided (4 ounces)

¼ cup julienned fresh basil leaves, plus extra for serving

SERVES 4

Spaghettoni is a thicker pasta than spaghetti, but you can also use regular spaghetti.

PREP AHEAD

Fill a large pot with water. Add 2 tablespoons of salt and bring to a boil.

Meanwhile, heat 3 tablespoons olive oil in a medium (10-inch) pot or Dutch oven, such as Le Creuset, over medium-low heat. Add the pancetta and sauté 5 to 7 minutes, until browned. Remove to a bowl with a slotted spoon and set aside. Add the onion and sauté for 10 minutes, until starting to brown. Add the reserved pancetta, the garlic, and red pepper flakes and cook for one minute. Add the wine and cook for 3 to 5 minutes, until the liquid has almost entirely evaporated. Add the tomatoes and sugar, bring to boil, lower the heat, and simmer uncovered for 10 minutes, stirring occasionally. Add 1 teaspoon salt and ½ teaspoon black pepper and taste for seasonings.

Meanwhile, add the pasta to the boiling water and cook for 2 minutes less than al dente according to directions on the package. With tongs, transfer the pasta to the pot with the sauce, bringing some of the pasta water with it. Cook over low heat for 2 minutes, stirring with the tongs and adding more pasta water as needed to make a loose sauce. Off the heat, stir in ½ cup of the Pecorino and the ¼ cup basil and toss with tongs. Taste for seasonings. Transfer to pasta bowls, sprinkle with the remaining ½ cup of Pecorino and more basil, and serve hot.

This recipe is inspired by one from Jamie Oliver, who's famous for fast, simple recipes. It's the essence of summer with bright lemon, fresh basil, and crunchy pine nuts, and it all comes together in no time at all.

lemon linguine with zucchini & basil

Kosher salt and freshly ground black pepper

2 medium zucchini, unpeeled, ends trimmed (about 14 ounces)

Good olive oil

½ pound dried linguine

1 tablespoon grated lemon zest

⅓ cup freshly squeezed lemon juice (2 lemons)

3 tablespoons unsalted butter, diced

¼ cup julienned fresh basil leaves

¼ cup freshly grated Italian Parmesan cheese, plus extra for serving

¼ cup toasted pine nuts (see note)

SERVES 4

To toast pine nuts, place them in a dry sauté pan over medium-low heat for about 8 minutes, stirring frequently, until lightly browned.

EASY

Fill a large pot with water, add 2 tablespoons salt, and bring to a boil.

Meanwhile, julienne the zucchini lengthwise on a mandoline. Heat 2 tablespoons of olive oil in a large (12-inch) sauté pan, add the zucchini, and cook over medium heat for 4 minutes, tossing occasionally. Turn off the heat and set aside.

Add the linguine to the boiling water and cook for 8 minutes, or 2 minutes less than al dente according to the instructions on the box. Transfer the pasta to the sauté pan with tongs, bringing some of the cooking water with the pasta. Add the lemon zest, lemon juice, butter, 2 teaspoons salt, and 1 teaspoon pepper.

Cook the pasta over medium-low heat for 2 minutes, adding more pasta cooking water as needed to make a loose sauce. Toss continuously to blend the pasta, butter, and cooking water. Off the heat, stir in the basil, Parmesan, and pine nuts. Sprinkle with salt and pepper and serve hot with extra Parmesan on the side.

I tested all kinds of hams—spiral-cut, bone-in, bone-out—and for me, Nodine's Woodland bone-in ham is the best. It's expensive but serves up to 20 people and it's so easy to prepare that I consider it money well spent. Pineapple juice, brown sugar, orange marmalade, and mustard make the most delicious glaze.

orange marmalade–glazed ham

1 (16 to 18-pound) bone-in smoked ham (not spiral-cut), such as Nodine's Woodland whole bone-in ham

1 cup canned pineapple juice

8 ounces orange marmalade, such as Tiptree

⅔ cup light brown sugar, lightly packed

½ cup ruby Port wine

½ cup Dijon mustard

¼ cup mango chutney, such as Stonewall Kitchen, plus extra for serving

Buttermilk Biscuits (page 205), for serving (optional)

SERVES 15 TO 20

TWO-FER: *Dice the leftover ham and add it to the Tuscan White Bean Soup (page 91), Overnight Mac & Cheese (page 157), or any of the egg dishes.*

CRAZY EASY

Allow the ham to stand at room temperature for one hour. With a long, sharp knife, cut off most of the dark outer layer on top of the ham, leaving all the fat. Score the fat diagonally in a diamond pattern without cutting down to the meat.

Meanwhile, preheat the oven to 300 degrees. Place the ham fat side up in a large, shallow roasting pan. Pour the pineapple juice over the ham and roast for 1 hour and 30 minutes.

Meanwhile, prepare the glaze. Combine the marmalade, brown sugar, Port, mustard, and chutney in a small saucepan. Bring to a boil over low heat, whisking to combine the ingredients, until the sugar has dissolved and the marmalade is melted. Set aside.

Spoon two thirds of the glaze over the ham. Raise the oven temperature to 325 degrees. Bake the ham for one hour, basting occasionally with the remaining glaze, until golden brown. Allow to rest for 15 minutes, slice, and serve hot or warm with the chutney and, if desired, with the biscuits.

vegetables & sides

Asparagus Cacio e Pepe

Balsamic Roasted Baby Peppers

Slow-Roasted Tomatoes with Fennel

Honey-Roasted Delicata Squash

Roasted Fingerling Potatoes
& Almost Any Green Vegetable

Glazed Sweet Potatoes

Easy Sesame Noodles

Brown Butter Skillet Cornbread

Molasses Baked Beans

Parmesan Polenta

Marble Potatoes with Garlic & Herbs

Maple-Roasted Honeynut Squash

Garlic-Roasted Haricots Verts

Parsnip Purée

Buttermilk Biscuits

all about roasting

Roasting is by far my favorite cooking method. When I'm cooking on top of the stove, every pot or sauté pan seems to need my constant attention. The bottom starts to burn so I need to stir it, the heat is too high and it boils over, or the heat is too low and it's not even simmering. It's anxiety-making.

But roasting is totally different. I can sear a piece of meat or fish in a sauté pan over high heat on top of the stove to get a good crust, then throw the whole pan in the oven to slow-roast completely unattended until it's full of flavor outside and juicy and perfectly cooked inside.

And it's not just meat that benefits from roasting; roasting is my preferred way to cook vegetables, too, not only for flavor but also because it's so much easier! We started roasting vegetables at my store, Barefoot Contessa, in the '80s when very few people were doing it. We would prep a huge amount of each vegetable in advance (you can do that, too!), then throw batches of them on sheet pans with olive oil, salt, and pepper and boom! They were ready to serve. And it was miraculous how much better they tasted than when we steamed or poached them. I mean, who likes boiled asparagus or Brussels sprouts???

A few tips about roasting: First, give your oven time to preheat properly. Before it's completely preheated, the temperature can fluctuate wildly. If, for example, you set the temperature to 400 degrees, it initially goes way past that, maybe as high as 450 degrees, before it cuts off. It can then drop as low as 350 degrees before the heat comes on again. Then it goes back up to 425 degrees, then down to 375, until it finally settles around 400 degrees. For most ovens, this process can take up to 30 minutes.

Second, use an oven thermometer. They're not very expensive at the hardware store and you'll be amazed how inaccurate the dial on your stove is. Sometimes I use two thermometers in the same oven at the same time, just to check that the oven thermometers are accurate. (I know, I'm obsessive!)

Third, don't use deep-sided pans. The sides on deep roasting pans keep the heat from circulating around the meat or vegetable so they don't roast evenly. The best equipment for roasting is, frankly, the least expensive—a sheet pan. I keep a stack of them so I can roast several things at the same time.

Finally, use the most flavorful, freshest vegetables for the best results. I've included recipes for standard vegetables like asparagus and broccolini but I've also included a few that are only available seasonally like Maple-Roasted Honeynut Squash (page 198) and Honey-Roasted Delicata Squash (page 180) to encourage you to search out less familiar heirloom varieties. And my Garlic-Roasted Haricots Verts (page 201) are so easy and addictive that you'll want to make them a lot.

One of my favorite recipes, though, is made with ingredients available year-round: Roasted Fingerling Potatoes & Almost Any Green Vegetable (page 185). You cut the unpeeled fingerlings in half, toss them on a sheet pan with olive oil, salt, and pepper, roast them until they're almost done, then throw whatever green vegetable you have around on top—broccolini, haricots verts, asparagus, sugar snap peas—and finish the roasting. Not only do you have a really good side dish; you have the vegetable and starch together in one dish!

I think you'll find that roasting makes your cooking, particularly vegetables, so much easier and more flavorful that you'll never go back to boiling them again!

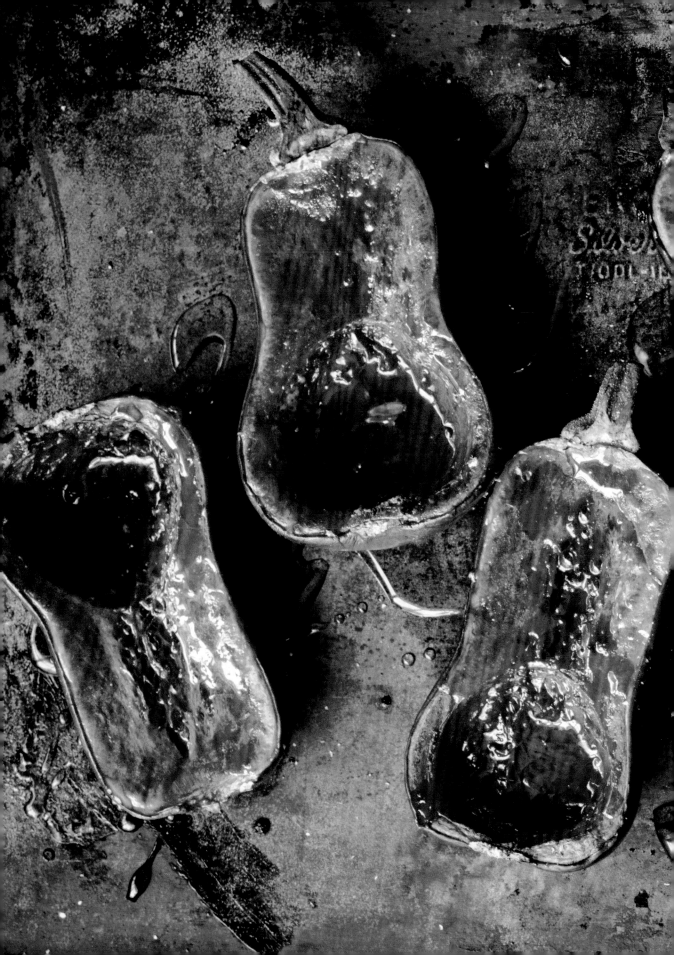

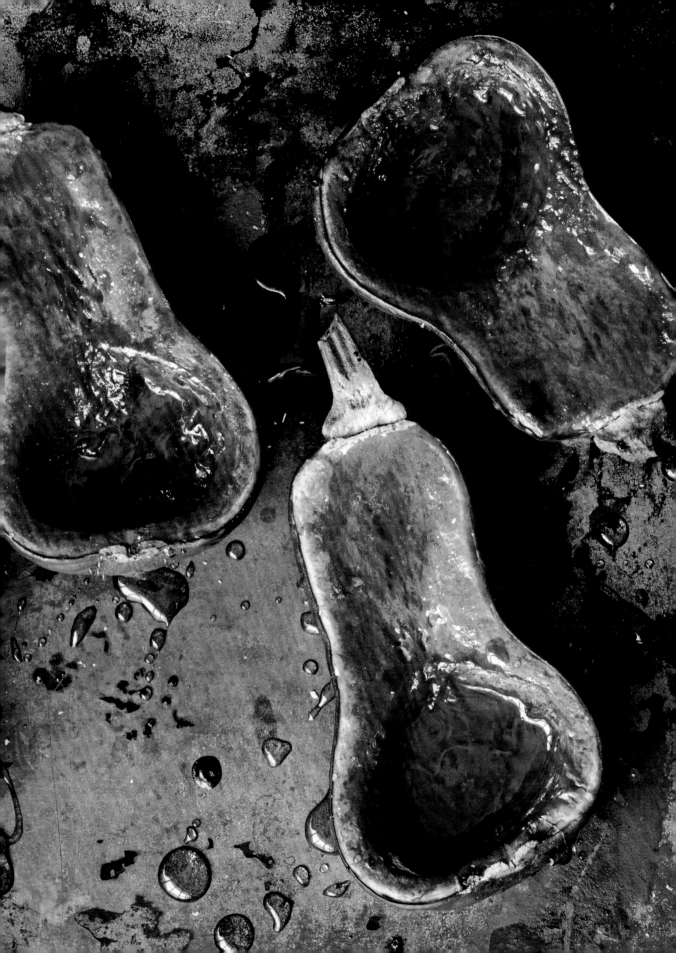

Asparagus is one of my favorite vegetables, so I'm always thinking of new ways to prepare it. Thick spears have the most flavor; taking the extra step of peeling the ends ensures they're tender when cooked. And butter, Pecorino, and Parmesan make everything taste better, right?

asparagus cacio e pepe

Kosher salt and freshly ground black pepper

1½ pounds thick asparagus spears

2 tablespoons (¼ stick) unsalted butter, melted

3 tablespoons freshly grated Italian Pecorino cheese

1 tablespoon freshly grated Italian Parmesan cheese

½ lemon

Fleur de sel or sea salt

SERVES 4

Preheat the oven to 450 degrees.

Place 12 cups of water and 2 tablespoons of kosher salt in a large pot, cover, and bring to a boil. Remove and discard the woody ends of the asparagus. Peel the bottom 2 inches of each spear with a vegetable peeler (see note). When the water boils, blanch the asparagus for 3 to 4 minutes, until they're just al dente. Drain.

Transfer the asparagus to a 10 × 13-inch rectangular baking dish. Add the butter, 1 teaspoon kosher salt, and ½ teaspoon pepper and toss to coat the asparagus. Arrange the asparagus decoratively in the dish, sprinkle with the Pecorino and Parmesan, and roast for 5 minutes, just until the cheese melts. Squeeze on the lemon juice, sprinkle with fleur de sel, and serve hot.

The peeler works best if you dip it in a glass of water from time to time.

EASY

TWO-FER: *Add leftovers to One-Pot Oven Risotto (page 158) or Warm Vegetable & Grain Bowl (page 98).*

When colorful baby peppers started showing up in my grocery store, I decided it would be great to just roast them whole. Just toss them—stems, seeds, and all—on a sheet pan with olive oil, salt, and pepper and you're good to go. Some syrupy balsamic vinegar at the end really enhances their flavor.

balsamic roasted baby peppers

2 pounds baby sweet peppers, mixed colors

Good olive oil

Kosher salt and freshly ground black pepper

2 sprigs fresh thyme

Aged balsamic vinegar, such as Villa Manodori

SERVES 6

Preheat the oven to 400 degrees.

Place the whole peppers, including the stems, in a single layer in a large (or two smaller) ceramic baking dish. Drizzle with 4 tablespoons olive oil, sprinkle with 2 teaspoons salt and 1 teaspoon pepper, and toss well. Lay the sprigs of thyme on top and roast for 20 to 25 minutes, until the peppers start to brown in places but are not blackened. Discard the thyme sprigs.

While still hot, drizzle the peppers with 3 tablespoons of balsamic vinegar and season to taste. Serve warm or at room temperature.

TWO-FER: *Add the cooked peppers to the Ploughman's Lunch (page 119) or remove the stems and seeds and add them to the Greek Orzo Salad (page 101).*

EASY

Roasting tomatoes at a low temperature over a long period of time concentrates their flavor and caramelizes the sugars. A sprinkle of fennel adds so much more flavor. This is an easy side dish that's great with any meat or poultry but even delicious served alongside Scrambled Eggs Cacio e Pepe (page 51).

slow-roasted tomatoes with fennel

2 pounds plum tomatoes

Good olive oil

¾ teaspoon fennel pollen or ground fennel (see note)

¼ teaspoon crushed red pepper flakes

Kosher salt and freshly ground black pepper

Fleur de sel or sea salt

SERVES 5 TO 6

Preheat the oven to 275 degrees.

Cut each of the tomatoes in half through the stem and place on a sheet pan. Drizzle with 3 tablespoons olive oil, sprinkle with the fennel, red pepper flakes, 1 teaspoon kosher salt, and ½ teaspoon black pepper. Toss with your hands and spread out in one layer, cut sides down. Roast for 2½ to 3 hours, until the cut sides start to brown around the edges.

Transfer the tomatoes to a platter, cut sides up, sprinkle with fleur de sel, and serve warm or at room temperature.

If you can't find fennel pollen or ground fennel, you can grind whole fennel seeds in a small coffee grinder (I keep one in the spice drawer just for grinding spices) or with a mortar and pestle.

EASY

Delicata squash started turning up at farm stands a while ago, and now some grocery stores carry them, too. The mild squash has a very autumnal flavor and it is so easy to cook because you don't even peel it. Oniony shallots, sweet honey, and sage give the roasted squash so much flavor!

honey-roasted delicata squash

2 pounds delicata squash, unpeeled

4 large shallots, peeled and cut in wedges through the root end

Good olive oil

2 tablespoons liquid honey

Kosher salt and freshly ground black pepper

2 tablespoons finely chopped fresh sage leaves

Fleur de sel

SERVES 4

Preheat the oven to 400 degrees.

Remove the ends of the squash, stand them upright, and cut in half lengthwise. Scoop out and discard the seeds, then cut the halves crosswise in ¾-inch-thick slices. Place the squash and the shallots in a large bowl. Combine ¼ cup of olive oil, the honey, 2 teaspoons kosher salt, and 1 teaspoon pepper in a small measuring cup. Stir in the sage, pour over the squash and shallots, and toss well.

Transfer the squash mixture to a sheet pan, spread out in a single layer, and roast for 20 to 25 minutes, until the squash is tender, turning once with a metal spatula.

Sprinkle with fleur de sel and serve warm.

EASY

When I go shopping I try to have a master recipe in my head like this one, which can be adapted to whatever seasonal vegetables are available. It's a good bet, because you can find fingerling potatoes all year long, and they pair just as well with snow peas in the spring as they do with veggies like broccolini.

roasted fingerling potatoes & almost any green vegetable

1½ pounds fingerling potatoes, cut in half lengthwise (see note)

3 large shallots, peeled and cut in wedges through the root end

Good olive oil

Kosher salt and freshly ground black pepper

6 to 8 large sprigs fresh thyme

1 pound broccolini, French string beans, broccoli, asparagus, snow peas, or other tender green vegetable

Sea salt or fleur de sel

SERVES 6

Preheat the oven to 400 degrees.

Place the potatoes (make sure they're dry) and the shallots on a sheet pan, drizzle with 4 tablespoons olive oil, sprinkle with 1½ teaspoons kosher salt and ¾ teaspoon pepper, and toss with your hands. Spread out in one layer, add the thyme branches on top, and roast for 25 to 30 minutes, turning once with a metal spatula, until the potatoes are tender and lightly browned. Discard the thyme branches.

Add the broccolini (or whichever green vegetable you are using) to the pan and toss with the potatoes. Roast for another 10 to 15 minutes (depending on the vegetable), until the green vegetable is crisp-tender. Sprinkle generously with sea salt and serve hot.

If you can't find fingerling potatoes, use 1-inch-diced Yukon Gold, white, or red new potatoes, unpeeled.

PREP AHEAD

Baking whole sweet potatoes takes a long time but dicing them and cooking them in a sauté pan takes no time at all. I add a little maple syrup and balsamic vinegar to enhance the sweetness of the potatoes themselves.

glazed sweet potatoes

1½ pounds sweet potatoes, peeled and ½ to ¾-inch diced (4 small)

Good olive oil

2 tablespoons (¼ stick) unsalted butter

Kosher salt and freshly ground black pepper

2 tablespoons pure maple syrup

Aged balsamic vinegar, such as Villa Manodori

Sea salt or fleur de sel

SERVES 4

Place the sweet potatoes, 2 tablespoons water, and 3 tablespoons olive oil in a large (12-inch) sauté pan. Cover and cook over medium heat for 5 minutes. Remove the lid, add 2 more tablespoons olive oil, the butter, 2 teaspoons kosher salt, and ½ teaspoon pepper and toss with the potatoes, spreading out in one layer. Sauté the potatoes uncovered over medium heat for 12 to 15 minutes, until tender, raising the heat at the end to reduce the liquid and tossing occasionally with a metal spatula.

Off the heat, drizzle the potatoes with the maple syrup and 2 teaspoons balsamic vinegar and toss well. Sprinkle with sea salt, taste for seasonings, and serve hot.

EASY

This complex-tasting sauce is from an old Barefoot Contessa recipe but so much easier to make. All you do is throw the ingredients into a blender and give it a good buzz. The sauce will last for a week in the fridge, so you can make sesame noodles for one dinner and serve it with grilled chicken another night.

easy sesame noodles

1 tablespoon coarsely chopped garlic (3 cloves)

2 tablespoons chopped fresh ginger

¼ cup vegetable or canola oil

¼ cup tahini, stirred

¼ cup creamy peanut butter, such as Skippy

¼ cup soy sauce, such as Kikkoman

¼ cup sherry vinegar

¼ cup dry sherry

2 tablespoons liquid honey

1 tablespoon toasted sesame oil

1 teaspoon chili paste or chili garlic sauce

Kosher salt and freshly ground black pepper

1 pound spaghetti, such as DeCecco

4 scallions, white and green parts, sliced diagonally

½ cup salted, roasted peanuts, roughly chopped

SERVES 6

Place the garlic and ginger in the jar of a blender. Add the vegetable oil, tahini, peanut butter, soy sauce, sherry vinegar, dry sherry, honey, sesame oil, chili paste, 1 teaspoon salt, and ¾ teaspoon pepper and process until puréed.

Bring a large pot of water with 2 tablespoons salt to a full boil. Add the pasta and cook al dente for 10 to 12 minutes (or according to the directions on the package). Transfer the spaghetti to a large serving bowl with tongs (don't drain it), bringing some of the cooking liquid with the pasta. While still hot, add enough sauce to coat the pasta and toss well. Add more cooking liquid, if necessary, to thin the sauce a little. Toss with the scallions and peanuts, sprinkle with salt, and serve warm or at room temperature.

Combine the pasta and sauce just before serving or the soy sauce will make the pasta mushy.

EASY / PREP AHEAD

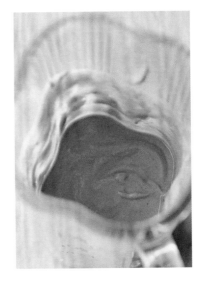

Melissa Clark of the New York Times *made a cornbread with brown butter and since I love cornbread, I decided to use that trick to update mine. This is the most delicious cornbread I've ever made!*

brown butter skillet cornbread

½ pound (2 sticks) unsalted butter

2¼ cups whole milk

2 extra-large eggs, lightly beaten

3 cups all-purpose flour

1 cup sugar

1 cup (fine) yellow cornmeal, such as Quaker

2 tablespoons baking powder

1 tablespoon kosher salt

Flaked sea salt, such as Maldon, for sprinkling

SERVES 10 TO 12

Preheat the oven to 350 degrees.

Melt the butter in a large (12-inch) round cast-iron skillet over medium heat. Continue to heat the butter until it's browned but not burnt (watch it very carefully!). Pour the butter and any brown bits into a medium bowl. Don't wipe out the skillet; just set it aside.

Whisk the milk into the butter, then whisk in the eggs until combined. (Don't add the eggs directly to the hot butter.)

In a large bowl, whisk together the flour, sugar, cornmeal, baking powder, and kosher salt. Make a well in the middle, pour the butter-and-milk mixture into the well, and stir with a rubber spatula *just* until combined. (Don't worry if it's a little lumpy.) Set the batter aside for 15 minutes to rest.

Stir the batter, transfer it to the skillet, and smooth the top. Sprinkle generously with flaked sea salt and bake for 25 to 30 minutes, until a toothpick inserted in the center just comes out clean. The top may crack. Cut in wedges and serve warm or at room temperature.

EASY

Erin French is the extraordinary owner/chef of the Lost Kitchen in Freedom, Maine. The baked beans recipe in her cookbook is the old-fashioned real thing; it has so much flavor and texture yet is not at all complicated to make.

molasses baked beans

1½ pounds dried cannellini or Great Northern white beans

½ pound pork belly (rind removed), ½-inch diced

½ pound slab smoked bacon, ½-inch diced

2 cups chopped yellow onions (2 onions)

1½ cups light brown sugar, lightly packed (see note)

½ cup ketchup, such as Heinz

½ cup molasses, such as Grandma's

½ cup pure maple syrup

2 tablespoons apple cider vinegar

1 tablespoon dry mustard, such as Coleman's

½ teaspoon crushed red pepper flakes

Kosher salt and freshly ground black pepper

SERVES 8

If your brown sugar has hardened, microwave it in the plastic bag for 30 to 60 seconds, until soft.

MAKE AHEAD

The night before you plan to cook, place the beans in a large bowl, add enough water to cover by 1 inch, and refrigerate overnight.

The next day, preheat the oven to 300 degrees.

Drain the beans and place them in a medium (10 to 11-inch) Dutch oven, such as Le Creuset. Add enough water to cover the beans by 2 inches, bring to a boil, lower the heat, and simmer uncovered for 45 to 50 minutes, until very tender. Skim off any foam that rises to the surface while they cook. Drain and return the beans to the Dutch oven.

Meanwhile, bring 4 cups of water to a boil. Heat a large (12-inch) sauté pan over medium heat and cook the pork belly and bacon together for 5 to 7 minutes, tossing often, until lightly browned. Remove to a plate with a slotted spoon and drain off all but 3 tablespoons of the fat. Add the onions and cook over medium-low heat for 5 to 7 minutes, stirring occasionally, until tender and lightly browned.

Add the onions and the reserved pork mixture to the beans along with the brown sugar, ketchup, molasses, maple syrup, vinegar, dry mustard, red pepper flakes, 4 teaspoons salt, and 1 teaspoon black pepper and combine. Pour in enough of the boiling water to *just* cover the beans, cover, and bake for 5 hours, checking the liquid level every hour. (If the beans are too dry, add a little more boiling water.) Remove the lid for the last 15 minutes so the beans turn a warm mahogany color. Check the seasonings and serve hot.

The polentas that I've made up until now were cooked on top of the stove and required lots of attention. This method from Paula Wolfert's memoir Unforgettable *is almost no-stir! It's creamy and delicious and cooks in the oven so you can set a timer and forget about it.*

parmesan polenta

4 tablespoons (½ stick) unsalted butter, divided, plus extra for the dish

1 cup (fine) yellow cornmeal, such as Quaker

2 cups good chicken stock, preferably homemade (page 83)

2 to 3 cups whole milk

Kosher salt and freshly ground black pepper

½ cup freshly grated Italian Parmesan cheese, divided

SERVES 4 TO 6

Preheat the oven to 350 degrees.

Grease an 11 × 9 × 2-inch oval baking dish with butter. Melt 2 tablespoons of the butter. In the prepared dish, combine the cornmeal, chicken stock, 2 cups of the milk, the melted butter, 2 teaspoons salt, and 1 teaspoon pepper. Bake uncovered for 45 minutes.

Remove from the oven and whisk the polenta until smooth, adding extra milk if it's too thick. Dice the remaining 2 tablespoons butter, distribute it on top, and bake uncovered for another 10 minutes.

Add ¼ cup of the Parmesan to the polenta and stir until smooth, adding more milk, ¼ cup at a time, if necessary. Sprinkle the remaining ¼ cup Parmesan and some pepper on top and serve hot.

Prepare the polenta completely, cool to room temperature, and refrigerate. To reheat, transfer the polenta to a medium saucepan, add water or chicken stock to thin it a little, and warm over medium-low heat, stirring occasionally, until hot and creamy.

EASY / MAKE AHEAD

This is the fastest roasted vegetable recipe I have ever made; the beans are ready in less than 10 minutes. They are the perfect side dish for almost any dinner, whether it's Wednesday night or Thanksgiving.

garlic-roasted haricots verts

1 pound French string beans (haricots verts), stem ends removed

Good olive oil

3 garlic cloves, grated on a Microplane

Kosher salt and freshly ground pepper

Freshly grated lemon zest, to taste (1 lemon)

SERVES 4 TO 6

Preheat the oven to 425 degrees.

Put the string beans on a sheet pan and toss them with 3 tablespoons olive oil, the garlic, 1½ teaspoons salt, and ½ teaspoon pepper. Spread them out on the pan and roast for 6 to 8 minutes, until crisp-tender and starting to brown on the bottom. Zest the lemon directly onto the warm beans and toss with a spatula. Sprinkle with salt and serve hot or warm.

EASY

This is about as easy as a side dish gets. Parsnips are really delicious and so underappreciated. My friend Julianna Margulies served us a simple parsnip purée that I became obsessed with. It's the essence of parsnip-ness with just a little butter. So good with any fish, meat, or poultry.

parsnip purée

1½ pounds parsnips, scrubbed and sliced ¾-inch thick

Kosher salt and freshly ground black pepper

2 tablespoons unsalted butter, diced

SERVES 4

Place the parsnips in a medium pot, add 1 tablespoon salt, and add enough water to cover the parsnips. Cover the pot, bring to a boil, then uncover, lower the heat, and simmer for 15 to 20 minutes, until the parsnips are very soft when tested with a small knife. Don't drain the pot!

With a slotted spoon or small strainer, transfer the parsnips to the bowl of a food processor fitted with the steel blade and pulse to chop the parsnips. Pour the cooking liquid into a glass measuring cup and pour ½ cup down the feed tube. Purée the parsnips, adding more cooking liquid (about 1 cup total) through the feed tube until the parsnips are creamy and almost smooth but still have some texture. Add the butter and ½ teaspoon pepper and purée until combined. Taste for seasonings and serve hot.

Prepare, refrigerate, and reheat on the stove, adding more liquid, if necessary.

EASY / MAKE AHEAD

The goal with biscuits is for them to be light and flaky but still moist. Buttermilk gives these biscuits great flavor and grating the cold butter instead of dicing it makes them very flaky. A sprinkling of sea salt before baking adds even more flavor.

buttermilk biscuits

2 cups all-purpose flour

1 tablespoon baking powder

Kosher salt

12 tablespoons (1½ sticks) cold unsalted butter, coarsely grated (see note)

½ cup plus 2 tablespoons cold buttermilk, shaken

1 cold extra-large egg

1 extra-large egg beaten with 1 tablespoon water or milk, for egg wash

Flaked sea salt, such as Maldon

MAKES 8 TO 10 BISCUITS

Preheat the oven to 425 degrees. Line a sheet pan with parchment paper.

Place the flour, baking powder, and 2 teaspoons kosher salt in the bowl of an electric mixer fitted with the paddle attachment. With the mixer on low, add the butter and mix **only** until combined.

Combine *all* the buttermilk and one egg in a small measuring cup and beat lightly with a fork. With the mixer on low, quickly add the buttermilk mixture to the flour mixture and mix just until all of the dough is moistened.

Dump the dough onto a well-floured board and knead quickly about 6 times. Roll the dough out ¾-inch thick. Cut with a 2½-inch round (not fluted) cutter and place on the prepared sheet pan. (You can reroll the scraps to make one or two more biscuits.) Brush the tops with egg wash, sprinkle with flaked salt, and bake for 20 to 22 minutes, until the tops are browned and the biscuits are cooked through. Serve hot or warm.

Grate very cold butter with a box grater (as you would carrots) onto parchment paper to move it easily. Dice any leftover pieces and add them to the dough.

PREP AHEAD / FREEZE AHEAD

TWO-FER: *Cut biscuit dough with a 1½- or 2-inch cutter and serve with Orange Marmalade–Glazed Ham (page 167).*

desserts

Panettone Bread Pudding

Dark Chocolate Tart

Vanilla Pound Cake

Lemon Meringue Squares

Bailey's & Cream

Rum Raisin Ricotta
Ice Cream

Fresh Berry &
Mascarpone Tart

Bourbon Chocolate
Pecan Pie

Beatty's Chocolate Cupcakes

Roasted Pineapple with
Coconut Gelato

Easy Chocolate Mousse

Cinnamon-Spiced
Shortbread

Dessert Board

store-bought is fine!

Several years ago, Jeffrey, some dear friends, and I took a vacation in France. It was October and we rented convertibles from a travel company that had already set the GPS in our cars for a great trip through Provence.

The trip started in the Luberon and wove through the beautiful hill towns of Ménerbes and Bonnieux. The GPS directed us to stop at a little café for coffee, to drive through fields of sunflowers, and along a beautiful ravine. At lunchtime, it suggested we stop at a little family restaurant. It was a dream guided tour of Provence but without the guide!

On the last day of the trip, we found ourselves in Cannes, home of the famed film festival. We found a little restaurant for lunch right on the beach (I mean literally, *on* the beach!) and we walked in to ask for a table. "*Mais non! Tout complet!*" (No! Totally booked!) We decided to have a drink at the bar and about five minutes later, the maître d' came over and said there was a table we could have. Yay!!

That restaurant was incredibly festive and the Provençal food was fresh and delicious. The music was cranked up and everyone was having a wonderful time, especially one very long table with a party of twenty young people. At the end of the meal, the waiters brought them a very, very long board filled with gorgeous desserts: tiny tarts, slices of French cake, cookies, fruit, and chocolates.

That display stopped me cold—especially when I realized that to re-create it, all I would have to do is buy some desserts from a bakery and arrange them on a board with fresh fruit. I've often said that "store-bought is just fine" about ingredients like frozen puff pastry but here was an entire dessert for twenty that could be totally "store-bought" and divine. It was a revelation!

I've included my rendition of that dessert in this chapter as a Dessert Board (page 245). Of course, you could add your own homemade Lemon Meringue Squares (page 222) or Beatty's Chocolate Cupcakes (page 233) but in a pinch, this will still be amazing even if you buy all the treats. Use your imagination and whatever delicious desserts you can find in your town. I hope it makes your dinner parties as fun as that lunch we had on the beach.

Panettone is an Italian sweet bread that is generally available only during the holidays. When you see it, snap some up, because it makes the best bread pudding! Any leftover panettone can be toasted and buttered for a weekend breakfast. I assemble the bread pudding early in the day, refrigerate it, and then bake it before dinner.

panettone bread pudding

1¼ pounds panettone (Italian sweet bread) (see note)

1½ tablespoons unsalted butter, melted

4 extra-large eggs

6 extra-large egg yolks

5 cups half-and-half

¾ cup granulated sugar

2 teaspoons pure vanilla extract

½ teaspoon grated orange zest

Kosher salt

⅓ cup sliced blanched almonds

Confectioners' sugar, for dusting

SERVES 8

Preheat the oven to 350 degrees.

Cut half of the panettone in ½-inch-thick slices and cut the rest into 1-inch dice. Place all of it on a sheet pan in a single layer and bake for 8 to 10 minutes, until lightly browned. Brush a 10 × 14 × 2-inch rectangular baking dish with the butter. Lay the sliced panettone in one layer in the dish, cutting the slices to fit, then distribute the diced panettone on top.

In a large bowl, whisk together the whole eggs, egg yolks, half-and-half, granulated sugar, vanilla, orange zest, and ½ teaspoon salt. Pour the mixture over the panettone, pressing lightly so the bread soaks up the custard. Set aside for 10 minutes or refrigerate for up to 6 hours.

Sprinkle the almonds on top, then place the baking dish in a large (13 × 16-inch) roasting pan. Fill the larger pan with enough very hot tap water to come halfway up the side of the baking dish, being careful not to get water in the pudding. Cover the larger pan tightly with aluminum foil, tenting it so the foil doesn't touch the pudding. Cut a few holes in the foil to allow steam to escape.

Bake the pudding for 45 minutes, then remove the foil and bake for 35 to 45 minutes longer, until a knife inserted in the center comes out clean. Carefully remove the baking dish from the water bath and cool slightly. Sprinkle lightly with confectioners' sugar and serve warm or at room temperature.

This will be delicious with either plain panettone with candied fruit or with chocolate panettone.

EASY / PREP AHEAD

This tart is adapted from Erin French's cookbook The Lost Kitchen *and it's the most luxurious chocolate dessert I've ever made. Instead of making a tart shell, this crust is made like a graham cracker crust but with chocolate wafers. The filling is like chocolate mousse with chocolate ganache on top. Crunchy salt brings out all the flavors. This is a wow dessert!*

dark chocolate tart

FOR THE CRUST:

1 (9-ounce) box Nabisco Famous Chocolate Wafers

¼ cup sugar

6 tablespoons (¾ stick) unsalted butter, melted

FOR THE FILLING:

6½ ounces bittersweet chocolate, such as Lindt, finely chopped (about 1 cup)

1¼ cups heavy cream

2 extra-large eggs, lightly beaten

1 teaspoon pure vanilla extract, such as Nielsen-Massey

FOR THE GLAZE:

3 ounces bittersweet chocolate, such as Lindt, finely chopped (about ½ cup)

¼ teaspoon instant coffee granules

¼ cup heavy cream

½ teaspoon flaked sea salt, such as Maldon

MAKES ONE 9-INCH TART

If either chocolate-and-cream mixture doesn't melt completely, heat in a microwave for 15 seconds, then stir well.

MAKE AHEAD

If you'd like to serve with a sauce, make a quick crème anglaise by melting vanilla ice cream and drizzling a puddle on the plate before plating each wedge of the tart.

Preheat the oven to 350 degrees.

For the crust, place the chocolate wafers and sugar in the bowl of a food processor fitted with the steel blade and process until finely ground. Pour into a medium bowl and stir in the butter. Press the mixture evenly into the bottom and sides of a 9-inch tart pan with a removable bottom. Place on a sheet pan and bake for 10 minutes. Set aside.

Meanwhile, for the filling, place the 6½ ounces of chocolate in a medium bowl. Heat the 1¼ cups cream in a small saucepan until it just comes to a boil. Pour the cream over the chocolate, allow it to stand for one minute, then stir gently with a whisk until smooth (see note). Stir in the eggs and vanilla, whisking until smooth. Pour into the crust and bake for 18 to 20 minutes, until the filling is set on the edge but still jiggly in the middle. Set aside to cool.

For the glaze, put the 3 ounces of chocolate and the coffee granules in a small bowl. In the same saucepan, heat the ¼ cup cream just to a boil and pour it over the chocolate. Allow to sit for one minute, then whisk until smooth. Gently pour the glaze over the chocolate filling (not the crust) and spread to the inside edge of the crust with a knife or offset spatula. Sprinkle with the sea salt and set aside at room temperature until set. Remove the rim of the tart pan and transfer to a flat serving plate. Cut in wedges (the crust may crumble a little) and serve at room temperature.

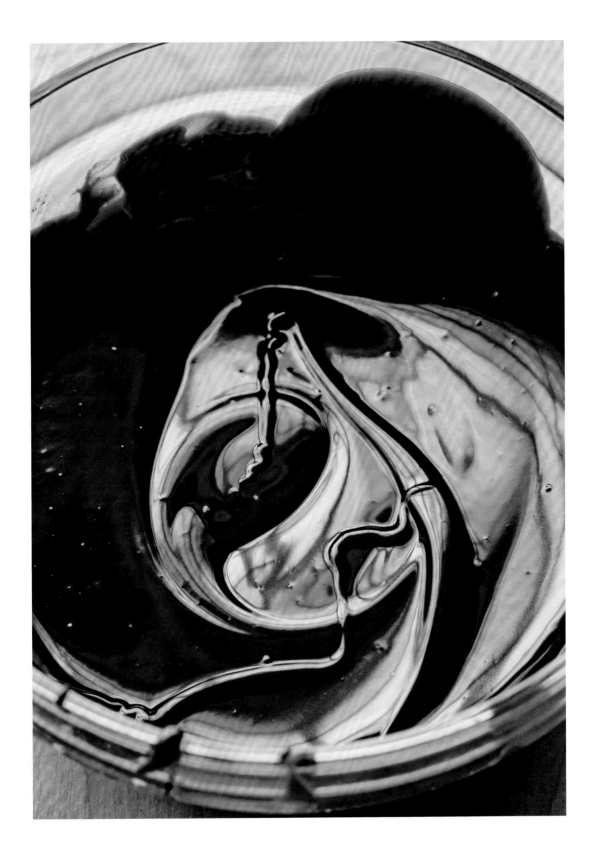

A good pound cake is a thing of beauty—simple but moist, with a fine texture and a complex flavor. Perfecting the recipe has been like a science project for me; once I added Cognac and lemon zest to the vanilla, I found I had achieved the ideal balance of flavors.

vanilla pound cake

⅓ cup turbinado or demerara sugar, such as Sugar in the Raw

3 cups sifted cake flour (not self-rising) (see note)

Kosher salt

½ pound (2 sticks) unsalted butter, at room temperature

2½ cups granulated sugar

6 extra-large eggs, at room temperature

2 tablespoons Cognac, Armagnac, or other brandy

2½ teaspoons pure vanilla extract

Seeds of 1 vanilla bean

1 teaspoon grated lemon zest

1 cup heavy cream

MAKES 2 LOAVES

Sift the flour **before** *measuring it.*

If your kitchen is cooler than 72 degrees, soften the butter for a few seconds in a microwave.

Allow to cool completely. Wrap twice with plastic wrap and refrigerate for up to a week or freeze for up to 4 months. Defrost overnight in the fridge.

TWO-FER: *Toast a slice and serve it with butter and Fresh Strawberry Rhubarb Preserves (page 64).*

MAKE AHEAD

Preheat the oven to 350 degrees. Grease two (8½ × 4½ × 2½-inch) loaf pans with butter. Sprinkle with the turbinado sugar, tilting the pans to make an even coating of the sugar on the bottom and sides.

Combine the flour and 1 teaspoon salt and set aside. In the bowl of an electric mixer fitted with the paddle attachment, beat the butter and granulated sugar on low speed, then raise to medium and beat for 5 minutes, until the mixture is light and fluffy. With the mixer on medium-low, add the eggs one at a time, beating to incorporate each egg fully before adding the next one. (Scrape down the beater and bowl as needed.)

Combine the Cognac, vanilla extract, vanilla seeds, and lemon zest in a small bowl and, with the mixer on low, add to the batter. (It might appear curdled at this point, which is fine.) With the mixer still on low, add the flour mixture and cream, alternately in thirds, beginning and ending with the flour and scraping down the bowl to combine. Beat on medium speed for 1 minute.

Divide the batter evenly between the prepared pans, smooth the tops, and bake for 45 to 50 minutes, until a toothpick inserted in the center comes out clean. (The tops will crack, which is fine.)

Cool in the pans for 15 minutes, remove from the pans, place on a baking rack, and cool completely.

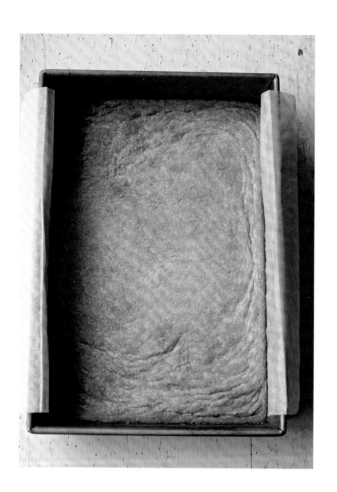

This has all the qualities of a great lemon meringue pie but is so much simpler to prepare. The crust and filling can be made days ahead and refrigerated separately, then assembled with the meringue topping just before baking.

lemon meringue squares

FOR THE CRUST:

12 tablespoons (1½ sticks) unsalted butter, at room temperature

½ cup sugar

½ teaspoon pure vanilla extract

1½ cups all-purpose flour

Kosher salt

FOR THE FILLING:

1½ cups sugar

3 tablespoons all-purpose flour

1 tablespoon cream of tartar

4 extra-large eggs

6 extra-large egg yolks (reserve the whites)

4 teaspoons grated lemon zest

1 cup freshly squeezed lemon juice (4 to 6 lemons)

6 tablespoons (¾ stick) unsalted butter, cut in 12 pieces

FOR THE MERINGUE:

6 extra-large egg whites

1 teaspoon cream of tartar

¾ cup sugar

SERVES 12

A 2-inch-wide metal spatula is helpful for getting the bars out of the pan.

MAKE AHEAD

The squares are also good served cold. Keep them in the pan and wrap them well. Refrigerate for up to a week.

Preheat the oven to 350 degrees. Butter a 9 × 13-inch metal baking pan.

For the crust: In the bowl of an electric mixer fitted with the paddle attachment, mix (don't whip) the butter and the ½ cup sugar until combined. Stir in the vanilla and 1 tablespoon warm water. In a separate bowl, combine the flour and ¼ teaspoon salt. With the mixer on low, slowly add the flour mixture and mix until it's in big crumbles. Transfer it to the prepared pan and pat it evenly in the bottom of the pan, covering it completely. Bake for 20 to 22 minutes, until the crust is nicely browned. Set aside, leaving the oven on.

For the filling: Place the 1½ cups sugar, the flour, cream of tartar, and ½ teaspoon salt in a large (8-inch) saucepan. Whisk in the eggs and egg yolks, lemon zest, and lemon juice. Cook over medium to medium-low heat for 10 to 12 minutes, until thick, stirring constantly with a wooden spoon. Off the heat, stir in the butter and set aside.

For the meringue: In the bowl of an electric mixer fitted with the paddle attachment, beat the egg whites, cream of tartar, and a pinch of salt on high until light and foamy. Reduce the speed to low, slowly add the ¾ cup sugar, then increase the speed to high and beat for 2 to 3 minutes, until the whites are glossy and form stiff peaks.

To assemble: Spread the filling over the crust, then spread the meringue over the filling, covering it completely. Swirl the meringue with a spoon to make lots of peaks. Bake for 10 to 20 minutes, until the meringue is nicely browned. Cool on a baking rack for at least 2 hours. Cut into 12 bars.

I always need a dessert in my repertoire that requires no cooking but is still really special. We spent a wonderful "day at the office" testing numerous combinations of creamy ice cream, icy sorbets, and sweet liqueurs, and this won hands down.

bailey's & cream

4 scoops good vanilla ice cream, such as Häagen-Dazs

4 scoops good coffee sorbet, such as Talenti Cold Brew Coffee Sorbetto

Bailey's Irish Cream liqueur

Toasted chopped pecans

SERVES 3 TO 4

Soften the ice cream and sorbet in a microwave until it's scoopable but not melted. Place one large scoop of vanilla ice cream and one or two large scoops of coffee sorbet in each bowl. Pour on the Bailey's Irish Cream and sprinkle each dessert with toasted pecans. Serve immediately.

If you can't find coffee sorbet, you can substitute coffee ice cream, but you won't get the same contrast in textures that you'll have with ice cream and sorbet together.

EASY / ASSEMBLED

This ice cream was inspired by a recipe on the wonderful Food52 website. Most ice creams require you to make a custard; for this one you purée all the ingredients in a food processor, chill the mixture, and freeze it in an ice cream maker. The ricotta gives it lots of creamy texture and the rum-soaked raisins are, well, rum-soaked raisins—which is to say delicious!

rum raisin ricotta ice cream

¾ cup golden raisins

½ cup dark rum, such as Mount Gay

15 ounces (1⅔ cups) fresh whole-milk ricotta

3 ounces cream cheese, diced (see note)

1 cup sugar

1 teaspoon pure vanilla extract

¼ teaspoon pure almond extract

Kosher salt

1 cup cold heavy cream

MAKES 4 TO 5 CUPS

Place the raisins and rum in a small saucepan. Bring the mixture to a boil over medium heat, remove from the heat, cover, and set aside until cool. Drain the raisins, reserving the rum.

Put the ricotta, cream cheese, sugar, vanilla and almond extracts, ⅛ teaspoon salt, and the reserved rum in the bowl of a food processor and pulse just until well blended. With the food processor running, pour the heavy cream down the feed tube and process until well blended. Pour into a quart container and refrigerate for at least an hour and up to a few days.

Pour the mixture into an ice cream maker and freeze according to the manufacturer's directions. When the ice cream is almost frozen, add the raisins and mix just to combine. Transfer to a container and freeze until firm. To serve, soften slightly and scoop into serving dishes.

Use regular (not whipped) cream cheese.

MAKE AHEAD / FREEZE AHEAD

Homemade tarts are always impressive to serve but even I get in a panic when it comes to rolling out tart dough. Instead, I make a shortbread crust that I just pat into the pan before baking. The mascarpone filling with Grand Marnier and Cognac is so good with the fresh berries on top.

fresh berry & mascarpone tart

FOR THE PASTRY:

12 tablespoons (1½ sticks) unsalted butter, at room temperature

½ cup sugar

Kosher salt

½ teaspoon pure vanilla extract

1¾ cups all-purpose flour

FOR THE FILLING:

16 to 18 ounces Italian mascarpone cheese

½ cup sugar

1½ tablespoons Grand Marnier

1 teaspoon Cognac, Armagnac, or brandy

1 teaspoon pure vanilla extract

1 pint fresh strawberries, hulled and sliced ¼-inch-thick lengthwise

½ pint fresh raspberries

½ pint fresh blueberries

MAKES ONE 10-INCH TART

Preheat the oven to 350 degrees.

In the bowl of an electric mixer fitted with the paddle attachment, mix the butter, sugar, and ¼ teaspoon salt on low speed just until combined (don't whip it!). Add the ½ teaspoon vanilla and, with the mixer still on low, slowly add the flour and mix just until the dough starts to come together. If the dough is dry, add 1 tablespoon water. Transfer to a 10-inch-round tart pan with a removable bottom and press into the bottom and sides of the pan (see note). Refrigerate for 15 minutes.

Butter one side of a 12-inch square of aluminum foil and place it, buttered side down, directly on the pastry. Fill the foil with pie weights, dried beans, or rice. Bake for 20 minutes, remove the foil and weights, prick the tart all over with a fork, and bake for 15 to 20 minutes, until the crust is lightly browned. Set on a rack to cool.

For the filling, place the mascarpone, the ½ cup sugar, Grand Marnier, Cognac, and the 1 teaspoon vanilla in the bowl of an electric mixer fitted with the paddle attachment and mix on medium-high speed, until smooth and slightly fluffy. Remove the rim of the tart pan, transfer the tart shell to a flat serving plate, and spread the filling evenly in the shell. Arrange the berries artfully on top. Serve at room temperature.

I use a metal measuring cup to press lightly on the dough for an even crust.

You can assemble the tart a few hours ahead and leave it at room temperature.

PREP AHEAD / MAKE AHEAD

This is a classic Kentucky Derby pie. You can certainly make a homemade pie crust, but I actually found that a store-bought crust is so much easier and oddly, it doesn't distract from the richness of the filling. Chocolate, bourbon, and pecans—what's not to love??

bourbon chocolate pecan pie

½ cup light brown sugar, lightly packed

½ cup granulated sugar

½ cup all-purpose flour

Kosher salt

8 tablespoons (1 stick) unsalted butter, melted and slightly cooled

2 extra-large eggs

1 teaspoon pure vanilla extract

2½ tablespoons good bourbon, such as Maker's Mark

1¼ cups semisweet chocolate chips, such as Nestlé's

1 cup whole pecans, large-diced

One (9-inch) store-bought frozen pie crust (see note)

Good vanilla ice cream, such as Häagen-Dazs, for serving

SERVES 6 TO 8

Preheat the oven to 350 degrees. Place an oven rack in the center of the oven.

In a medium mixing bowl, combine the brown sugar, granulated sugar, flour, and 1 teaspoon salt. In a smaller bowl, whisk together the butter, eggs, vanilla, and bourbon. Pour the liquid ingredients into the dry ingredients and stir with a rubber spatula until combined. Stir in the chocolate chips and pecans.

Place the pie crust on a sheet pan lined with parchment paper. Crimp the edge with a floured fork, pour the filling into the pie crust, and smooth the top. Bake for 35 to 40 minutes on the prepared rack until the filling is evenly golden brown on top and as firm in the middle as it is at the edges.

Transfer to a wire rack to cool completely. Serve in wedges with a scoop of vanilla ice cream.

Defrost frozen pie crust overnight in the fridge.

EASY

My friend Michael Grim's grandfather had a milk route in Pennsylvania Dutch country, and his grandmother Beatty baked chocolate cakes for him to deliver with the milk. I published her recipe in Barefoot Contessa at Home *but so many people have asked if the cake can be made into cupcakes that I decided to test it. Not only can it, these are now my go-to cupcakes. The recipe works well as a sheet cake, too!*

beatty's chocolate cupcakes

1¾ cups all-purpose flour

2 cups sugar

¾ cups good unsweetened cocoa powder (see note, page 235)

2 teaspoons baking soda

1 teaspoon baking powder

Kosher salt

1 cup buttermilk, shaken

½ cup vegetable oil

2 extra-large eggs, at room temperature

1 teaspoon pure vanilla extract

1 cup freshly brewed hot coffee

Chocolate Buttercream (recipe follows)

MAKES 24 CUPCAKES

To freeze the cupcakes, refrigerate first to firm the icing, then wrap with plastic wrap and freeze.

For a sheet cake, grease and line a 9 × 13-inch baking pan with parchment paper, then grease and flour the paper. Pour the prepared batter into the pan and bake for 30 minutes. Cool. Prepare a half recipe of the Chocolate Buttercream and spread it on the cooled cake.

EASY / MAKE AHEAD

Preheat the oven to 350 degrees. Grease the tops of two 12-cup muffin pans, line all the cups with paper liners, and set aside.

Sift the flour, sugar, cocoa, baking soda, baking powder, and 1 teaspoon salt into the bowl of an electric mixer fitted with the paddle attachment. Mix on low speed until combined. In another bowl, combine the buttermilk, oil, eggs, and vanilla. With the mixer on low, slowly add the wet ingredients to the dry ones. With the mixer still on low, add the coffee and stir just to combine, scraping the bottom of the bowl with a rubber spatula. (The batter will be very liquid.)

Divide the batter among the prepared muffin cups (I use a standard 2¼-inch ice cream scoop). Bake for 25 minutes, until a cake tester inserted in the center of a cupcake comes out clean. Cool in the pans for 30 minutes, then turn them out onto a cooling rack and cool completely.

Pipe or spread the Chocolate Buttercream onto each cupcake. Store covered at room temperature (don't refrigerate) and serve at room temperature.

chocolate buttercream

12 ounces good semisweet chocolate, such as Valrhona (see note)

1 pound (4 sticks) unsalted butter, at room temperature

2 extra-large egg yolks, at room temperature

2 teaspoons pure vanilla extract

2½ cups sifted confectioners' sugar

2 tablespoons instant coffee powder

GENEROUSLY FROSTS 24 CUPCAKES

Chop the chocolate and place it in a heatproof bowl set over a pan of simmering water. Stir until just melted and set aside until cooled to room temperature.

Beat the butter in the bowl of an electric mixer fitted with the paddle attachment on medium-high speed until pale and fluffy, about 3 minutes. Add the egg yolks and vanilla and continue beating for 3 minutes. Turn the mixer to low, gradually add the confectioners' sugar, then beat on medium speed, scraping down the bowl as needed, until smooth and creamy. Dissolve the coffee powder in 2 teaspoons of hot tap water. On low speed, add the chocolate and coffee to the butter mixture and mix until blended. Don't whip it!

For the cake I use Valrhona cocoa powder, and for the buttercream I use Valrhona Le Noir 56% Cacao Semisweet Chocolate. You can use any good semisweet chocolate.

My friend Elsa Walsh served me this amazing dessert, her improvisation on a recipe from Ferran Adrià's cookbook The Family Meal. *If you can find them, golden pineapples are truly sweeter than the regular variety. The lime zest and coconut sorbet add the perfect balance of flavors.*

roasted pineapple with coconut gelato

1 large (5 pound) ripe golden pineapple

6 tablespoons light agave syrup

2 limes

1 to 2 pints coconut gelato, such as Talenti Caribbean Coconut

SERVES 4 TO 5

Preheat the oven to 400 degrees.

Cut off the top and bottom of the pineapple and stand it upright. With a sharp knife, remove the rind by cutting strips from top to bottom, making sure you remove all the brown spots or "eyes." Cut the pineapple in quarters lengthwise through the core, and then cut each quarter again in half **lengthwise** through the core. Lay each piece on its side and remove the core. Place the pineapple on a sheet pan in one layer and roast for 20 minutes. Cool to room temperature.

Cut the pineapple crosswise in ½-inch-thick pieces and transfer them to a bowl. Add the agave and the zest of 2 limes, using a Microplane to zest the limes directly into the bowl to capture the oils. Toss well.

Spoon the pineapple and the juices into dessert bowls, place a scoop of gelato on top, sprinkle with extra lime zest, and serve.

EASY

Making an old-school chocolate mousse takes time but this one is so much easier. It's full of flavor from two kinds of chocolate with lots of coffee and Kahlúa to balance the sweetness. It's also great for entertaining because it's totally make-ahead.

easy chocolate mousse

8 ounces bittersweet chocolate, chopped, such as Lindt

4 ounces milk chocolate, chopped, such as Lindt

¼ cup freshly brewed espresso or strong coffee

¼ cup Kahlúa

½ teaspoon pure vanilla extract

2 extra-large organic egg yolks, at room temperature

4 extra-large organic egg whites, at room temperature (see note)

Kosher salt

½ cup cold heavy cream

⅓ cup sugar

Sweetened Whipped Cream, for serving (recipe follows)

SERVES 4 TO 5

Place the bittersweet chocolate, milk chocolate, and espresso in a large heatproof bowl set over a pan of simmering water. Heat just until the chocolates melt, stirring occasionally. Off the heat, whisk in the Kahlúa and vanilla and set aside to cool for 15 minutes. Whisk in the egg yolks, one at a time, until combined.

Meanwhile, in the bowl of an electric mixer fitted with the whisk attachment (you can also use a hand mixer), beat the egg whites and a pinch of salt until they form soft peaks. Whisk half of the egg whites into the warm chocolate mixture and then fold in the remaining egg whites using a rubber spatula. Without cleaning the bowl or whisk, beat the cream and sugar together on high speed until they form soft peaks. Gently fold into the chocolate mixture until there are no white streaks.

Pour the mixture into a 6-inch-round × 3-inch-high soufflé dish or four or five (10-ounce) glass bowls and chill for at least 2 hours or overnight. Spoon or pipe the Sweetened Whipped Cream on top and serve cold.

I recommend using organic eggs for this recipe because they're not cooked.

MAKE AHEAD

sweetened whipped cream

¾ cup cold heavy cream

1½ tablespoons sugar

¾ teaspoon pure vanilla extract

SERVES 4 TO 5

Place the cream, sugar, and vanilla in the bowl of an electric mixer fitted with the whisk attachment (you can also use a hand mixer) and beat on high speed until the cream forms stiff peaks.

I love shortbread in any form but this one with cinnamon and "apple pie" spices is extra special. The basic shortbread dough was inspired by my friend Eli Zabar, of EAT in New York City. Not only are these cookies delicious but the house smells wonderful when you make them!

cinnamon-spiced shortbread

¾ pound (3 sticks) unsalted butter, at room temperature

1 cup sugar

1 teaspoon pure vanilla extract

3½ cups all-purpose flour

2 teaspoons ground cinnamon

Kosher salt

FOR THE SUGAR COATING:

½ cup sugar

½ teaspoon ground cinnamon

½ teaspoon ground nutmeg

¼ teaspoon ground cloves

MAKES 16 TO 20 COOKIES

Preheat the oven to 350 degrees. Line two sheet pans with parchment paper.

In the bowl of an electric mixer fitted with the paddle attachment, mix together the butter, the 1 cup sugar, vanilla, and 1 tablespoon warm water on low speed until they are just combined (don't whip it!). In a medium bowl, sift together the flour, the 2 teaspoons cinnamon, and 1 teaspoon salt. With the mixer still on low, slowly add the flour mixture to the butter mixture, mixing just until the dough comes together in large clumps. Transfer to a floured surface and shape into a flat disk. Wrap in plastic and chill for just 30 minutes.

Roll the dough ½ inch thick on a floured board and cut with a large (3½-inch) star cutter or any other shape you like! Place the cookies one inch apart on the prepared sheet pans and bake for 20 to 22 minutes, until the edges just begin to brown.

Meanwhile, for the sugar coating, combine the ½ cup sugar, cinnamon, nutmeg, and cloves in a medium bowl. As soon as the cookies come out of the oven, sprinkle them thickly with the sugar mixture and allow to cool on the sheet pans. When the cookies are cool, shake off the excess sugar mixture and serve warm or at room temperature.

Prepare the dough and cut out the cookies, then refrigerate or freeze in containers. Bake and sprinkle with the sugar mixture before serving.

Wrap the baked cookies and store at room temperature for several days.

MAKE AHEAD

dessert board

No dinner, including a Breakfast-for-Dinner, is complete without dessert. If the meal is light, it's nice to serve something a little decadent for dessert, but if the dinner is rich and filling, I prefer to make something fruity and light. I don't want my guests going home feeling like they never want to eat again!

But then there is the easiest dessert of all to serve—a Dessert Board. On a wooden board, I arrange a really colorful assortment of pastries and cakes from a local bakery plus gorgeous, big strawberries and green grapes and maybe big shards of chocolate bark to finish it off. That way, everyone has something they love for dessert and my guests can choose whether they want to eat something light or something rich—or maybe both!

Here are suggestions for what to assemble but be creative; as long as the shapes and colors are different from each other they will make a beautiful dessert board.

Brownies and bars

Cookies

Cupcakes

Small fruit tarts

Sliced cake, such as pound cake

Long-stemmed strawberries

Fresh figs

Bunches of green grapes

Dried fruit

Caramels

Shards of chocolate bark with nuts or dried fruit

ASSEMBLED

resources

Roman and Williams Guild
53 Howard Street
New York, New York 10013
Premium home décor and furniture
rwguild.com

Bloom
25 Madison Street
Sag Harbor, New York 11963
Antiques, hostess gifts, tableware
monaatbloom@gmail.com (no
website)

Monc XIII
40 Madison Street
Sag Harbor, New York 11963
Mid-century and new furniture
monc13.com

CB2
979 Third Avenue
New York, New York 10022
Modern home furnishings
cb2.com

Williams Sonoma
Kitchenware and home furnishings
williams-sonoma.com

Crate&Barrel
Home décor and kitchenware
crateandbarrel.com

The Lost Kitchen
Kitchenware, pantry, and tableware
findthelostkitchen.com

To peel or not to peel?

When I write a recipe, I always try to be clear yet concise about how ingredients should be prepped. I assume people know how to prep common vegetables. For example, I'll just simply write "2 yellow onions, chopped" because I assume you know you need to peel it first. Likewise, fingerling potatoes and English cucumbers are generally **not** peeled. Therefore, I would only add a note about prepping if I want you to do something **other** than what you would normally do, as when I note in the recipe for Homemade Chicken Stock (page 83) "1 head garlic, unpeeled" or "1 carrot, scrubbed." And while I assume butternut squash is always peeled and seeded, I specify "unpeeled" for delicata squash, which you may not have cooked before and would not know that the skin is completely edible.

Here is a list of common vegetables and how I expect they'll be prepped for use in my recipes. Any time I deviate from these rules, it will be noted where the vegetable appears in the ingredient list. I hope this helps answer any of your questions.

Vegetables you'll **always** peel before slicing or chopping, unless otherwise noted:

RUSSET POTATOES

GARLIC

PARSNIPS

CELERY ROOT

YELLOW ONIONS

TRADITIONAL CUCUMBERS

CARROTS

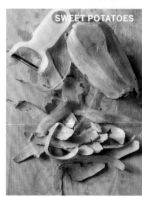
SWEET POTATOES

Vegetables you *don't* peel before slicing or chopping, unless otherwise noted:

BUTTERNUT SQUASH

TURNIPS

DELICATA SQUASH

RED ONIONS

BABY POTATOES

EGGPLANTS

FRESH GINGER

HOTHOUSE CUCUMBERS

MARBLE POTATOES

SHALLOTS

ZUCCHINI

BELL PEPPERS

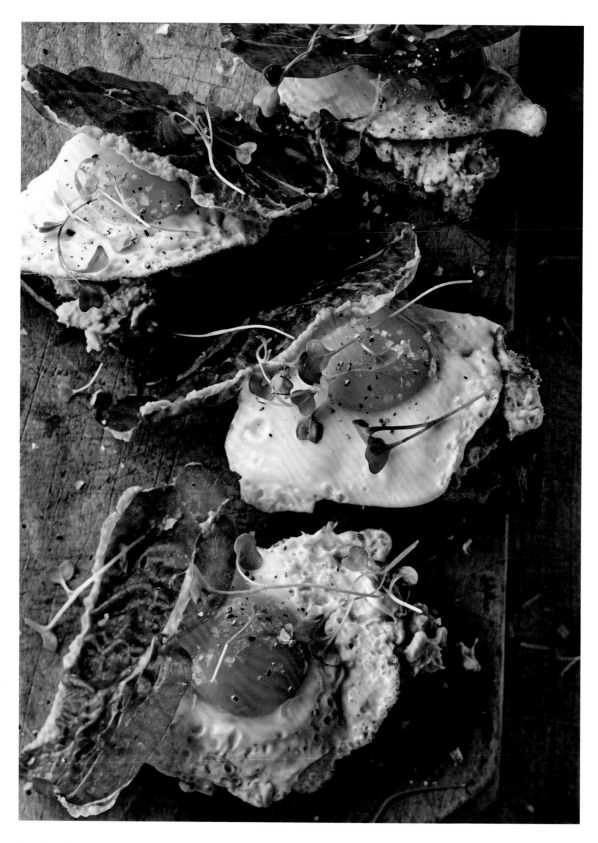

AVOCADO & FRIED EGG TARTINES, PAGE 59

index

recipe index